EVIDENCE
EMBALMED

EVIDENCE EMBALMED

MODERN MEDICINE AND THE MUMMIES OF ANCIENT EGYPT

EDITED BY

ROSALIE DAVID

AND

EDDIE TAPP

MANCHESTER
UNIVERSITY PRESS

© A. R. David and E. Tapp 1984

Published by Manchester University Press
Oxford Road, Manchester M13 9PL
and 51 Washington Street, Dover,
New Hampshire 03820, USA

British Library cataloguing in publication data
Evidence embalmed
   1. Manchester Museum   2. Manchester
Mummy Team   3. Mummies — Radiography
I. David Rosalie   II. Tapp, E.
393'.3'0932   DT62.M7

Library of Congress cataloguing in publication data
Evidence embalmed
   Bibliography: p. 166
   Includes index.
   1. Mummies — Egypt — Addresses, essays, lectures.
2. Mummies — Egypt — Radiography — Addresses, essays,
lectures.   3. Egyptians — Diseases — Addresses, essays,
lectures.   4. Manchester Museum (University of Manchester)
— Addresses, essays, lectures.   I. David, A. Rosalie
(Ann Rosalie)   II. Tapp, E. (Edward)
DT62.M7M78   1984   932   84-2649

ISBN 0-7190-1079-9
ISBN 0-7190-1082-9 Pbk

Typeset in Linotron 202 by
Graphicraft Typesetters Limited, Hong Kong
Printed and bound in Great Britain by
Riddles Ltd, Guildford and King's Lynn

CONTENTS

To Alan Warhurst, MA, FSA, FMA, Director of the Manchester Museum, in gratitude for his support and encouragement of our endeavours, from the members of the Manchester Egyptian Mummy Research Team.

ACKNOWLEDGEMENTS

We would like to express our thanks to the following for their support and co-operation:

The Vice-Chancellor of the University of Manchester; the Chairman and members of the Manchester Museum Committee and the Director of the Museum; members of the museum staff; the British Academy for several grants towards our research, the Wellcome Trust who provided financial help for the symposia and Kodak Ltd, for a most generous supply of film; the staff of all the departments and institutions of the University who have been involved with the work. Special thanks are due to the staff of the Department of Neuroradiology at Manchester Royal Infirmary and to the Director and staff of the Department of Medical Illustration. At Preston Royal Infirmary, we are grateful to Miss Anna Krypczyk and the staff of the Histology Department, and to Mrs Pamela Thompson and the staff of the Neuro-pathology Department.

For the fieldwork in Egypt, we wish to extend our warmest gratitude to Dr Ahmed Kadri, chairman of the Egyptian Antiquities Organization, for granting the concession to examine the skeletal remains recovered from Cheops' necropolis; and to Dr Ali El-Khouli and Mr Nassef Mohammed Hassan for facilitating its issue. The author of chapter 6 is indebted to Mr J. Holmes for the translation of the relevant passages in Junker's archaeological reports, and to Chicago University Press for permission to quote the concluding paragraph of the chapter written by J. R. Harris in *An X-ray Atlas of the Royal Mummies*. He is also grateful for the interest and inspiration of *Shemsu Kemet*.

Mr B. Norman, Head of History & Archaeology, BBC Television, and Mr J. Selwyn Gilbert, producer, and his colleagues who enabled some of the current research to be translated into a visually exciting film in the 'Chronicle' series, which was televised in 1983.

Dr A. E. Hanwell, author of 'Need to Save Money?', and Mrs J. Ovendon for typing some of the manuscripts.

To our publishers, Manchester University Press, we wish to express our gratitude for their encouragement and support, and particularly to thank Catherine Annabel who has guided the production from the beginning.

Finally, the team members would like to offer thanks and appreciation to the spouses who have provided inspiration and encouragement throughout the project.

A. Rosalie David
Manchester, 1984

NOTE ON THE CONTRIBUTORS

The following specialists, most of them members of the Manchester Mummy Team, contributed to this book:

Editors

A. Rosalie David, BA, PhD. Director of the Manchester Egyptian Mummy Project since its inception in 1973. Took a degree in Egyptology at University College London and proceeded to a PhD on religious ritual in ancient Egyptian temples at University of Liverpool. Has been the Egyptologist at the Manchester Museum since 1972. Also holds post of honorary lecturer in Comparative Religion in University of Manchester. Author of nine books on Egyptian history and religion, and the editor of two previous books about the Mummy project. Has contributed papers on the work of the project to various scientific journals, and has also lectured widely on the subject in Britain, USA, and Canada.

E. Tapp, MD, FRC Path., MRCS (Eng.), MRCP (Lond.). Qualified in medicine in 1959 and proceeded to a MD, Liverpool in 1964. Became a member of the Royal College of Pathologists in 1968 and was awarded the Fellowship of the College in 1980. Has held posts in the university departments of pathology in both Liverpool and Manchester and is now consultant in Histopathology and Morbid Anatomy at the District Laboratory, Preston Infirmary. Author of many articles on the pathology of cancer and other topics. During the past ten years has been an active member of the Manchester Mummy team and of the Palaeopathology Association, contributing to the two previous books published by the team and reading many papers both in this country and abroad on the pathology of Egyptian mummies and on a uniquely preserved body which he was asked to examine in 1981 by the Department of the Environment.

The other contributors are listed alphabetically:

R. A. Fawcitt, MB, ChB, DMRD, FRCR. Qualified in medicine at Edinburgh and held initial post in Sheffield. Now consultant radiologist in Department of Neuroradiology at Manchester Royal Infirmary.

G. Fildes, MB, ChB. Qualified in medicine in 1949 at the University of Manchester. Retired from general practice in 1984. Certificate in Egyptology, University of Manchester in 1977. Has assisted with the cataloguing of the Manchester Museum Egyptian Collection since 1975.

T. Flaherty, MB, BCh (NUI), MRCP (UK), MRC Path. Qualified in medicine in Cork in 1972. Became a Member of the Royal College of Physicians in 1975 and a Member of the Royal College of Pathologists in 1979. Has held posts as senior registrar in haematology in several Manchester hospitals and is now consultant haematologist at the Royal Preston Infirmary.

Detective Chief Inspector A. Fletcher. Until retirement in 1983, was the head of the Fingerprint Bureau and Scenes of Crime Department, Greater Manchester Police. Devised the special method for obtaining fingerprints from mummified tissue.

T. J. Haigh, FIMLS. Senior chief medical laboratory scientific officer in charge of the Blood Transfusion Department at the Royal Preston Hospital.

Professor I. Isherwood, MB, ChB, DMRD, MRCP, FRCR. Professor of Diagnostic Radiology, University of Manchester. Consultant neuror-adiologist, Manchester Royal Infirmary.

Hilary M. Jarvis HDCR. Superintendent radiographer in Department of Neuroradiology, Manchester Royal Infirmary.

A. Krypszyk, FIMLS. Senior chief medical laboratory scientific officer in charge of immunohistochemistry at Preston Royal Infirmary.

F. F. Leek, LDS, RCS, FSA, FRGS. Author of *The Human Remains from the Tomb of Tutankhamun*. Co-author of several books and author of many articles on scientific aspects of dentistry and Egyptology. Honorary member of the Swedish Academy of Medical Science, Dental Association of South Africa and the Sociedad Peruana de Ortodoncia. Member of team which, in 1968, examined the mummy of Tutankhamun. Has studied human remains from ancient Egypt in universities and museums in most capital cities of Europe and the Near East.

R. A. H. Neave, FMAA, AIMBI. Attended art school for formal training and later specialised in medical art at the Middlesex Hospital, London. Joined Manchester University in 1959 as medical artist. Now holds post of assistant director in the Department of Medical Illustration. Responsible for the reconstruction of the heads of three Egyptian mummies, including that of '1770'.

C. W. A. Pettitt, MSc, MIBiol, FLS. Assistant Keeper in Zoology, Manchester Museum. Has been concerned with the computerisation of collection data for some fifteen years, using the University computer facilities. Now controls the Museum Computer Cataloguing Unit, where the International Mummy Database forms one of the current projects.

P. Stanworth. Consultant neurosurgeon, Institute of Neurological Sciences, Glasgow.

Mrs P. Thompson, FIMLS. Senior chief medical laboratory scientific officer in the technical neuropathology department at Preston Royal Infirmary.

K. Wildsmith. From an engineering background, moved into a sales career. Currently a senior salesman with KMI (Keymed Industrial), selling remote visual inspection equipment. Became closely involved in Mummy project after KMI was approached for assistance in examining various mummies with endoscopic equipment.

PROLOGUE

On 10 June, 1975, in an operating theatre at Manchester University Medical School, an unusual event in the history of Egyptology took place. The specially invited audience, including members of the Press and television teams, watched with rapt attention as the first steps were taken in this investigation. For the 'patient', lying on the operating table, had been dead for thousands of years. The arc lights picked out with brilliant clarity the small figure, enclosed in layers of dull brown bandages, highlighting the gilded face mask with the inlaid artificial eyes. The unwrapping and dissection of this Egyptian mummy was the key-event of a major investigation of the collection of human and animal mummies held by the Manchester Museum. It was the climax of several years of painstaking research and investigation by a team of specialists – Egyptologists, medical experts and scientists – who brought together their skills and knowledge in the most extensive examination of its kind to have been carried out in Britain. The team gathered around, in green gowns and masks, as Dr Rosalie David, the Director of the project, removed the first bandages from the mummy.

Nearly seventy years earlier, Dr Margaret Murray, the first curator of Egyptology at the Manchester Museum, had unwrapped one of the mummies known as the 'Two Brothers' in the Chemistry Theatre of the University of Manchester, before a specially invited audience. But although radiological examinations of other collections of mummies had been carried out in the intervening years, no other mummy had been the subject of a multi-disciplinary autopsy and investigation in Britain. Thus, the unwrapping of this mummy (whose name was unknown and was therefore referred to by its museum accession number of 1770) was a rare and newsworthy event.

From 1973 until 1975, the other mummies in the collection (which consisted of seventeen human and thirty four animal mummies) had been investigated as thoroughly as possible, using a variety of non-destructive methods. These techniques included radiology, histo-pathology and electron-microscopy, dental examination, carbon-14 dating, scientific facial reconstruction, fingerprinting, and chromato-graphical identification of substances found in the associated bandages.

The Manchester Egyptian Mummy Project, as it was known, had a number of clearly defined aims. First, the team planned to discover as much information as possible from a specific group of mummies which could then be related to existing knowledge of religious and funerary beliefs and customs, living conditions, the state of physical and dental health and the process of mummification used in ancient Egypt. It was hoped that identifiable evidence of disease would be found in the bodies and their associated organs, and that, in some cases, it would be possible to pinpoint the probable cause of death. In addition, the team intended to establish a methodology, using many different techniques under near-ideal conditions for the examination of a group of Egyptian mummified remains, which other institutions could then adopt and adapt for the investigation of their own collections.

In 1979, the Manchester Project had completed the first phase of the research programme. An international symposium, entitled 'Science in Egyptology', was held at the University of Manchester, and scholars and scientists from four continents discussed the application of scien-tific techniques to the study of Egyptology and, in particular, to the mummified remains. A television programme was produced by the BBC in their *Chronicle* series, which looked at the work of the project, the unwrapping of 1770, and the follow-up research, against the wider background of Egyptian funerary beliefs and earlier attitudes towards mummies. Two short films were also produced by the Audio-Visual Service of the University of Manchester; one showed the major events in the unwrapping of 1770, while the other recorded the various methods and techniques which were employed in the examination of all the Manchester mummies. Intended for general use in teaching departments, the films have been widely shown in Britain and also abroad; the longer film, dealing with the techniques, was awarded the major film award of the British Association for the Advancement of Science for 'the most effective presentation to a non-specialist audience of a scientific or technological subject'. The other film was the winner of one of five certificates of merit presented by the same organisation.

A public exhibition, entitled 'O, Osiris, Live Forever!', which presented the results of the team's work against a background of Egyptian religious and funerary beliefs and customs, was also held in the Manchester Museum in 1979–80 and attracted a wide public response. In the 'Museum of the Year' awards for 1980, it received the Sotheby's Award for the best temporary exhibition in Britain. Subsequently, a selection of two-dimensional material and artifacts from this exhibition toured the country and formed the nucleus of an exhibition held at the University of Alberta, Edmonton, Canada, as part of the university's seventy-fifth anniversary celebrations.

By 1979, the first written accounts of the team's work had also appeared. A scientific book[1] detailed the aims, techniques and results of the processes, while a more general account[2] related the story of the unwrapping of 1770 and described the wide range of techniques used by the team.

It was then decided that the team would develope their techniques and research along various lines, building on the results of the last ten years. Techniques such as radiology and pathology – major diagnostic tools in the original survey – were developed in this second phase, and the Museum's acquisition of five additional human mummies provided new material for these studies. Secondly, techniques such as serology which had not been used in the original investigation were now brought in. New research in the field extended the scope of the project, when, on behalf of the Manchester Museum, F. Filce Leek undertook a programme of investigation of a major collection of dry skulls near the nobles' tombs at Gizeh, Egypt. Combined with previous studies he had made of collections of skulls in museums in Britain and Europe, this survey enabled Mr Leek to prepare a unique account of the dental profession in ancient Egypt, which is presented in this book. Another important aspect of the work at Manchester has been the development of virtually non-destructive techniques of investigating mummified remains; here, considerable advances have been made in the scientific reconstruction of wrapped heads, involving the use of x-rays, and in the employment of endoscopy as a means of obtaining tissue for histology, without unwrapping and dissecting the mummy.

Since 1979, when the idea was first proposed and accepted at the Manchester symposium, an International Mummy Data Base has been established at the Manchester Museum, designed first to gather and store information on disease discovered in Egyptian mummies, and secondly, to supply data to scholars on the occurrence and possible patterns of disease at different historical periods.

However, perhaps one of the most fascinating aspects of the work is the adoption in forensic studies of some of the techniques devised for use on the mummies. A technique of fingerprinting, specially devised for use on the Manchester mummies, has subsequently been introduced into the standard practices of some police forces, and the knowledge obtained from scientifically reconstructing the three-dimensional heads of three of the mummies has since been of benefit in the highly skilled work of plastic surgery.

It is these new concepts, techniques and applications which form the main subject of this present book, and, as in previous accounts, the story of the development and application of the techniques is written by the team who carried out this exacting but exciting task. As an introduction to this, a brief history of the development of mummification is given, and an outline of the fascinating story of the examination of mummies in Britain and elsewhere, from the 'unrolling' of mummies, brought back as souvenirs from Egypt, during the nineteenth century, to the first scientific investigations of mummies and the earliest radiological and paleopathological studies.

⟦Part I⟧
THE BACKGROUND

Fig 1.1 Coffin for a mummified cat. Late period,
c. 700 BC (Manchester Museum)

[[1]]

INTRODUCTION

Mummification in ancient Egypt

The meaning of 'mummy'   Today, the term 'mummy' is used to describe
any artificially preserved body in countries throughout the world.
However, to the general public, the word is almost invariably associated
with the wrapped and often elaborately decorated bodies of the ancient
Egyptians which lie in glass cases in major museums. The word
'mummy' is in fact derived from the Persian word 'mumia', meaning
bitumen or pitch. According to Abd' al-Latif,[3] an Arab physician and
writer of the twelfth century AD, 'mumia' was a substance that flowed
down from the tops of mountains and, mixing with the waters that
carried it down, coagulated like mineral pitch. The 'Mummy Mountain' in Persia was famous for the black, bituminous matter which
oozed from it and which was credited with medicinal and healing
properties. Indeed, in 1809, the Queen of England received a present of
this precious substance from the King of Persia. Preserved bodies from
ancient Egypt, particularly those of the Ptolemaic period (332–30 BC),
often have a blackened appearance. It was later wrongly assumed that
this was the result of soaking the body in bitumen, and thus, the idea
seems to have arisen that these embalmed bodies would provide an
alternative source of bituminous material to the natural exudation.
Since it resembled 'mumia' in appearance, it was presumed that it had
the same properties and could be used as effectively in medicines.
Therefore, the Persian word 'mumia' came to be applied to the
preserved bodies of the Egyptian dead, and today they are universally
known as 'mummies'. However, the use of the word as a medical
ingredient continued well into the nineteenth century AD, and a brown

pigment, also derived from fragments of these bodies, and used in oil painting, was similarly known as 'mummy brown'.

Ancient sources   Apart from the evidence provided by the mummified bodies, we must turn to Greek rather than Egyptian sources for a detailed account of the techniques of mummification. There are no ancient Egyptian illustrations of the process, although series of tomb scenes show various stages in the burial rites. No Egyptian literary source provides technical details of the procedure, although some religious allusions to the concept of mummification occur in funerary texts such as the Pyramid Texts, the Coffin Texts and the Book of the Dead, while other papyri detail some of the rituals associated with embalming.

However, our most complete accounts are given by Greek writers who described many facets of life in Egypt, in the works of Herodotus[4] who lived in the fifth century BC, and Diodorus Siculus,[5] writing some four hundred years later. Passing references occur in other classical sources, but these do not consider the techniques used in mummification. We must therefore rely upon the writings of Herodotus for most of our information, with the minor variations and additions given by Diodorus Siculus. However, some caution must be exercised in accepting the complete validity of these accounts; Herodotus doubtless received much of his information from the priests, and he was writing in a relatively late period, thousands of years after the greatest times of Egypt's history – the Old, Middle and New Kingdoms – when mummification was at its peak. Techniques must have varied over the years and what was true of the fifth century BC was not necessarily valid for earlier periods, although the basic principles of evisceration and dehydration by means of natron to arrest decomposition apparently remained constant.

Nevertheless, using these accounts, a general picture of the process of mummification can be obtained. The body of the deceased was brought by his family to the embalmers, who were a special, hereditary class in Egypt. They showed wooden models to the relatives who, according to their means, selected one of the three available methods of preservation. The cheapest method, used to prepare the bodies of the poorer classes, was simply to rinse the body through with a purge, to preserve it for seventy days, and then to return it to the family. The second method was to fill the belly of the corpse with cedar oil by means of a syringe, the body being plugged to prevent the escape of the oil. After an appointed number of days, the cedar oil was released from the body, bringing with it the liquified organs and bowels; the body was then returned to the family. The third and most expensive method was inevitably the most elaborate. The brain was drawn out through the nose, partly with a hooked iron and partly by use of medicines which liquified the brain. An incision was made with 'a sharp Ethiopian knife' in the side of the abdomen and the viscera were removed, except for the heart (believed to be the seat of the emotions and intellect) and the kidneys. The viscera were cleaned with palm wine mixed with various spices, and treated with natron.[6] They were then either placed in canopic jars or packed in bandages and returned to the body cavities. The body was cleansed and rinsed through with palm wine and crushed incense; it was then filled with crushed myrrh, cassia and other spices, and sewn up again. Natron was then used to preserve the body, although there has been some controversy about the method actually employed. The ambiguity of one of the words in Herodotus' text at first led scholars to infer that the bodies were immersed and soaked in baths of natron, but recent experiments have shown that it is most likely that the bodies were packed with dry natron, and that the alternative translation of the word should be accepted. The preservation process continued for not longer than seventy days. The body was then washed again and wrapped in strips of fine linen cloth which had been coated with gum. Amulets were inserted between the wrappings, to bring magical protection to the deceased, the relevant religious rites were performed, and finally, the mummy was returned in its wooden coffin to the family for the final burial ceremonies.

In recent years, experiments have been carried out which have attempted to simulate the techniques described in the literary sources, with the aim of determining the degree of accuracy of the ancient accounts. Pioneering work was done in this field by A. Lucas, and further research has been performed by Z. Iskander. In the Manchester project, R. C. Garner's experiments on a series of dead rats indicated that the most expensive method of mummification did in fact produce the best results in terms of stability and appearance. A period of thirty or forty days was found to be the maximum required to produce a stable condition in an animal treated with dry natron alone, perhaps indicating that the Egyptians themselves used only this time for the treatment with natron, utilising the remainder of the seventy day period quoted by Herodotus for anointing the body with oils and for religious rites. The Manchester experiments also indicated that several factors probably affected the final condition of the body after mummification. These included the use of too little natron or frequent use of the same natron which would reduce its effectiveness as a dehydrating agent; variations in the composition of the natron (i.e. the percentage of impurities in it) which would have caused some variation in effectiveness; the stage of decomposition which the body had reached when it first arrived at the embalmers' workshop; and, in the later historical periods, a decline in professional standards amongst the embalmers became apparent, as religious motives for mummification were obscured and the process became more widely available than ever before amongst the lower social orders.

History of mummification   Mummification, or the artificial preservation of the body after death, was practised in Egypt from the Old Kingdom (*c.* 2686–2181 BC) down to the Christian era. It eventually died out with the Arab invasion and conquest of Egypt in the seventh century AD. However, its origins probably go back to the beginnings of Egypt's religious awareness, and we can glean something of the beliefs and customs which perhaps originally inspired the people with a strong desire to preserve the bodies of their dead in as enduring and lifelike a state as possible.

    Egypt is a land of dramatic contrasts – the Nile is its *raison d'être* and its life-force, and whereas in the north the river fans out into the fertile triangle of land known as the Delta, in the Nile valley itself the green, cultivated strip which stretches away on either side of the river must be created and maintained by constant irrigation and ceaseless vigilance. This fertile land gives way abruptly to the desert, regarded by the ancient Egyptians as a hostile environment, symbolising death whereas the cultivation represented fecundity and life. Because the agricultural land was so scarce, supporting the people, their animals and their crops, the Egyptians chose not to bury their dead here, near their towns and villages, but to dispose of the corpses in the desert sands that fringed the cultivation. Probably devised as the earliest method of disposal, dating back to the predynastic period (before 3100 BC), this almost certainly had a profound effect upon their later religious and funerary developments.

    The naked body, perhaps covered by a reed or skin mat, was placed in a shallow grave in the sand at the edge of the desert. This primitive procedure continued in use for the poorer classes throughout the dynastic period (c. 3100–332 BC) although it was supplanted by mummification for the wealthier people. Almost certainly by accident, this presented the Egyptians with one way of preserving the body after death, and the germ of at least some of their ideas probably developed from seeing these long-dead, desiccated but well-preserved bodies when they were exposed in the shallow graves, which were laid bare by the action of marauding jackals who roamed the burial sites or the movements of wind-blown sand. The environmental conditions combined to preserve these bodies indefinitely: the dryness of the sand and the hot, rainless climate quickly dried out the newly-buried corpse, and the body fluids were absorbed into the sand. This process arrested decomposition, and produced remarkable desiccated bodies which can still be seen in some museums. The skin and hair are present, often in an excellent state of preservation, and although these cannot strictly be classified as 'mummies', such bodies undoubtedly inspired the subsequent attempts at artificial preservation.

One of the most distinctive aspects of the ancient Egyptian civilisation is the clearly defined belief in a continued human existence after death. This permeated and influenced many facets of their society. Of central importance to the belief of a continuing and individual life after death was the equally potent concept that this was, at least in part, dependent upon the preservation of the deceased's body in as lifelike a form as possible. The individual personality was regarded as complex and many-faceted; some elements, such as the *Ba* (soul) and the *Ka* (spirit), were considered to be immortal, perpetuating the individuality of the deceased after death. However, the *Ka* was thought to return periodically after death, to partake of the food and drink offerings placed at the tomb, and thus gain spiritual sustenance. In order to do this, the *Ka* needed to make use of the preserved body, or mummy, in the tomb, which, if it still closely resembled the person when alive, could be readily recognised by the *Ka*.

These religious beliefs must already have been established in the earliest historical periods, but at the same time, in the archaic period (c. 3100–2686 BC), increasingly sophisticated attitudes had also developed towards the disposal and burial of the dead. The royal family and the great nobles began to construct deeper and more elaborate tombs, lined with wood or mud-brick, and often covered with a superstructure above ground. The tombs were filled with household goods and food for use in the afterlife, and the deceased was often enclosed in a wooden coffin. But this meant that the body was no longer in direct contact with the hot, dry sand, which had been the means of preserving the predynastic bodies. As a result, decomposition of the body tissues became a serious problem, for a preserved body was now regarded as an essential element for existence in the afterlife. It thus became necessary to find an alternative method of preserving the lifelike form and features of the deceased.

Some fifty years ago, the archaeologist Quibell[7] discovered human remains in the second dynasty cemetery at Saqqara. These exhibited features which were probably early attempts at mummification. A large mass of corroded linen was discovered between the outer bandages and the bones of a mummy; this may have been an attempt to use crude natron, or some other substance, as a preservative by applying it to the surface of the body. Although few satisfactory mummies are preserved from the archaic period and the early part of the Old Kingdom, the surviving evidence suggests that a type of 'stucco' mummy was produced. The earlier loose body-cover was replaced by close-fitting linen bandages, which emphasised the body contours. The limbs were wrapped separately; facial features, the breasts and the genitalia were moulded in bandages impregnated with a gummy substance and details were added in paint. Underneath the bandages, however, the body continued to decompose. The end result was an elaborately wrapped and moulded skeleton, and a successful method of mummification still had to be found.

A good example from the Old Kingdom of the development of this early type of mummy is the body (probably fifth dynasty) which was discovered at Medum by Sir William Flinders Petrie in 1891. This was later presented to the Royal College of Surgeons in London. It showed that an attempt had been made to recreate the facial features and the organs with resin-soaked linen, while at the same time endeavouring to preserve the body tissues. The German scholar, Junker, and the American, George Reisner, discovered mummies which displayed similar features. Covered first with fine linen, the bodies were then enclosed in stucco-plaster, and every attempt was made to depict the body features in detail, paying special attention to the head.

Evisceration of the body – a major advance in the technique of mummification – was performed, at least for members of the royal family, as early as the fourth dynasty. This was a deliberate attempt to prevent decomposition and to preserve the body tissues, rather than creating a modelled likeness on the body. The discovery of the canopic chest belonging to Queen Hetepheres, the wife of Sneferu and mother of Cheops who built the Great Pyramid, contained viscera removed from the queen's body after death.

In general terms, it is likely that the contracted position of burial was abandoned around the time of the third dynasty and bodies were subsequently buried in the extended position, lying on the left side. In turn, this was replaced by the dorsal position, from the New Kingdom onwards.

During the Middle Kingdom (1991–1786 BC), various changes occurred. More examples are preserved than from the Old Kingdom, but the results were generally less successful. Some were found by Maspero while he was excavating at Thebes in 1883, and de Morgan discovered others at Dahshur. An important group were brought to light by Naville in 1903, while he was excavating the eleventh dynasty mortuary temple of Nebhepetre Mentuhotep II at Deir el-Bahri. He discovered the tombs of the princesses, and the mummies, examined by Derry, showed no trace of a flank incision for removal of the viscera, but provided tentative evidence of partial evisceration *per anum*. An American expedition working in the same area ten years later found several other mummies of royal princesses, and again, preservation seems to have been achieved by the injection of resinous material into the alimentary canal *per anum*. These are of great importance, indicating how mummification was carried out for the royal family at this period.

Generally, however, the preparation of the bodies was less painstaking and the results are less successful. Although it was now customary in non-royal persons to remove the viscera (lungs, liver, stomach, and intestines) through an incision made in the left side of the abdomen, less attention was given to the actual preservation of the body tissues. Usually a thin coat of resin was applied to the surface of the skin; this left desiccation (the drying out of the body) incomplete so that decomposition soon set in. Therefore, although great care was lavished on the outward appearance of the mummies, inside the wrappings there is usually only a jumble of bones with little remaining soft tissue.

Nevertheless, the Middle Kingdom saw the rise to importance of the non-royal person. Whereas, in the Old Kingdom, the afterlife was the exclusive prerogative of the king, and others could only hope to achieve a vicarious continued existence after death through the king's bounty, now in the Middle Kingdom, the democratisation of religious and funerary beliefs became widespread. Centred around the worship of the god Osiris, who promised eternity to all his followers regardless of wealth or rank, the new beliefs gained rapid popularity. Gradually, the nobility, and all those who could afford the expenditure, adopted the funerary customs once reserved for the royal family. They built and equipped fine tombs, and all those involved in the making and preparation of funerary goods found their trade flourishing. Mummification was adopted by new sections of the society, although the relative expense involved ensured that the mass of the population continued to be buried simply in the desert graves. Even to the poorest, however, the cult of Osiris offered hope of an individual and blessed eternity in the god's own kingdom, if the worshipper had lived a good and worthy life.

Several types of funerary equipment were now introduced, or older forms were transformed for use by a wider market. The use of containers for the mummified viscera – known as canopic jars – now became widespread. These jars, always four in a set, and made of stone, pottery or wood, were dedicated to the 'Four Sons of Horus', who were demi-gods with special responsibility for the safe-keeping of the organs. Before the eighteenth dynasty, the stoppers of the jars were all carved in the form of human heads, but after this, only one, representing Imset, was shown thus. He protected the liver. The jar dedicated to Hapy, who was responsible for the lungs, had an ape-headed stopper, while the stomach was placed in the jar belonging to Duamutef, with a jackal-headed stopper. The fourth jar, with the hawk-headed stopper, represented Qebehsenuef who looked after the intestines. The heart remained *in situ*, except in cases where it had been wholly or partly severed because of careless manipulation by the embalmer. No satisfactory explanation can be given for the practice of leaving the kidneys in the body. 'Canopic' is the term which early Egyptologists applied to these jars and the chest which housed them. They mistakenly connected them with the Greek legend of Canopus, the helmsman of Menelaus, who was buried at Canopus in the Delta and was worshipped there in the form of a jar.

A particularly fine example of a Middle Kingdom tomb-group is to be seen in the Manchester Museum. Discovered at Rifeh in Middle

Fig 1.2 The anthropoid coffins of the Two Brothers,
c. 2000 BC (Manchester Museum)

Egypt, the two mummies (Museum nos. 21470 and 21471) date to c. 1900 BC and are known as the 'Two Brothers'. They were unwrapped in Manchester in 1908 by Dr Margaret Murray and the subsequent scientific investigation provided valuable information regarding the techniques of mummification. Very little skin tissue remained on the bodies and two very different methods of mummification were employed. The coffin inscriptions provide the information that they were both sons of a woman named 'Aa-Khnum', but the paternal history is not given and, since the two men exhibit markedly different racial physiques, it has been suggested that they may have had different fathers. One, Nekht-Ankh, was about sixty years of age at death; according to custom, his viscera were removed, dehydrated and stored separately in a set of canopic jars. The other, Khnum-Nakht, who probably died in early middle age, has a less well-preserved mummy and no accompanying set of jars. The present project has made a further study of the human remains of the brothers and has produced some interesting pathological and other conclusions.

The period between the Middle and New Kingdoms, known as the second intermediate period (1786–1552 BC), was a troubled time for Egypt. Invaded and ruled by foreign dynasts, the Hyksos, the country was finally restored to native rulership by the princes of Thebes, who established the eighteenth dynasty. Not surprisingly perhaps, little evidence of mummification practices has emerged from this period. However, the body of one of these warring Theban rulers, named Seqenenre, has been found. The physical evidence indicates that the body was cursorily mummified probably near the bettlefield where Seqenenre fell, for it is apparent that he died from a severe head wound. No attempt was made to place the body in the usual extended position, and although the viscera were removed, the brain was not. Indeed, the contorted arms, hands and face still bear witness to his agonising death.

In the New Kingdom, for the eighteenth to twentieth dynasties (1552–1087 BC) a more abundant and continuous set of mummies is available for study. Two caches of royal mummies were found at Thebes between 1881 and 1898 AD, which provide a great deal of information, for, although they represent only one section of society, they can be identified and arranged in chronological order; thus, other non-royal mummies of this period can be compared with them, and dated accordingly.

An innovation introduced in this period was the removal of the brain.

There is no positive evidence for this before the eighteenth dynasty, but from King Ahmosis I, who ruled at the start of the eighteenth dynasty, the custom is established. Various methods of extraction were developed, but the most common was to force an instrument up the nostril and drive it right through the ethmoid bone. The brain was then removed in pieces from the cranial cavity, probably using a ladle, and although most was extracted, fragments of brain can be found in some skulls. The empty skull was then packed with resin-soaked strips of linen.

The positioning of the hands of the mummies varied according to sex and period. There were exceptions, but generally the mummies of females had their hands alongside their thighs, while men's arms were fully extended with the hands turned inwards at the side of the thighs. In the mummy of Tuthmosis II (1501–1491 BC), however, the arms were crossed over the chest, and this custom was adopted until the twenty-first dynasty when the arms were once again placed in the extended position. Nail-covers were attached to the fingers to ensure that the nails were not lost during embalming. The incision for the removal of the viscera was placed lower in the side of the mummy of Tuthmosis III (1490–1436 BC), another practice which continued until the twentieth dynasty. The mummy of the obese pharaoh, Amenophis III, who ruled towards the end of the eighteenth dynasty, shows an attempt to restore the lifelike contours of the body by means of subcutaneous packing, with the introduction of stuffing under the skin of the legs, arms and neck. This simulation of the king's plumpness when alive is the earliest example of a technique which was to become commonplace in the twenty-first dynasty.

The nineteenth dynasty (1308–1194 BC) produced some fine examples of mummification. The excellent state of preservation of the head of King Sethos I enables us to judge the quality of the embalmer's skill. In the mummy of his son, Ramesses II, an advance can be observed in the technique which preserved the natural colouring of the skin, in contrast to the blackening and discolouration usually evident in earlier mummies. At the end of this dynasty and the beginning of the next, there was a period of experimentation when the early steps were taken towards the advanced techniques of the twenty-first dynasty.

Mummification was at its most skilful during the twenty-first dynasty. At this period, the badly desecrated royal mummies of the previous three dynasties were partially restored and re-buried, and this may have made the embalmers aware of their predecessors' failure to preserve the lifelike appearance of the rulers. Every attempt was now made to preserve the body and, of equal importance, to reproduce the body contours and lifelike features of the individual. Two methods of retaining this appearance were available:the external application of padding materials to the body surface, a method which had been tried with some success in the Old Kingdom; and the insertion of packing materials under the skin surface, which had been attempted once before, in the mummy of Amenophis III. It was this second method which the embalmers now sought to develop, so that the mummy could be identified as closely as possible with the deceased.

Since a number of royal and priests' mummies from this period were available for study, Sir Grafton Elliot Smith[8] was able to examine them in detail, and from his observations, it was possible to determine the distinctive features of the new method. The viscera, removed through an incision in the left side, were no longer stored in canopic jars, but were packed into four separate parcels, and inside each was placed a figurine representing one of the 'Sons of Horus'. These parcels were then returned to the body cavities, with other packing material. The heart was still left *in situ* in the body. The removal of the brain was still practised, and there were several methods of cerebral extraction but the most common was via the nasal passage.

The body was now restored to its original contours. The body cavity was packed through the wound in the left side, and, in addition to the viscera parcels, packing materials included sawdust, butter, linen and mud; to prevent escape, the wound was plugged with linen. The contours of the body were simulated by introducing packing under the skin through a series of small incisions made in its surface. The neck and cheeks were also packed, with the face stuffing being introduced through the mouth.

The mummy was also identified with the deceased by the insertion of artificial eyes in the orbits, made of limestone, calcite or bone, or sometimes, balls of linen with the pupils delineated in black paint. The face and sometimes the complete body were painted with red ochre (for men) and yellow ochre (for women); and the natural hair was augmented with false tresses. From the evidence for this period, it seems to be customary that male and female royal mummies had their hands placed alongside their hips, while the mummies of the priestly class had their hands over the genital organs.

Fig 1.3 Reed coffin enclosing a mummified baby. From Gurob, *c.* 1500 BC (Manchester Museum)

The mummy which shows the transitional stage from the old to new techniques is that of Queen Nodjme, wife of Herihor. Here, the older method of building up the body by means of external packing is used and there is no attempt to introduce the elaborate subcutaneous packing, but the face is packed, through the mouth, with sawdust, and artificial eyes have been inserted.

The innovations of the twenty-first dynasty were retained in the twenty-second and twenty-third dynasties, but after that the standards of mummification gradually declined and more attention was given to the exterior wrapping of the mummy than to its internal preservation. By the twenty-sixth dynasty, subcutaneous packing had been mainly abandoned, the viscera were no longer returned to the body and the parcels were simply placed between the legs or, once again, were stored in canopic jars which were revived as a major element of funerary equipment.

Several mummies in the Manchester collection date to the New Kingdom (eighteenth–twentieth dynasties – 1552–1087 BC) and the third intermediate period (twenty-first–twenty-sixth dynasties – 1087– 525 BC). From the nineteenth dynasty, there is the mummy of a priest of Amun, named Khary (no. 9354); this was brought to England in its decorated coffin in 1893, when it was said to be the oldest passenger transported to Manchester arriving via the ship canal. The only example in the museum collection of a poor person's burial (no. 3496) also dates to the New Kingdom. It is a child, wrapped in a reed mat tied with ropes at either end, and comes from Gurob, an eighteenth dynasty town-site.

Four female mummies date to the third intermediate period; two examples are of the twenty-first dynasty: the mummy of Ta-ath (no. 10881), brought probably from Luxor by a member of the Frewen family of Sussex, and the Parr mummy (no. 1976.51A), with its painted wooden coffin. The other mummies date to the twenty-fifth dynasty: Asru (no. 1777), complete with two decorated wooden coffins, had already been unwrapped before arrival in the museum in 1825, as the first Egyptian accession of importance. This mummy probably came from Luxor, and she had the title 'Chantress of Amun'. Well preserved and of considerable medical interest, Asru has featured prominently in the team's research. The other mummy, named Perenbast (no. 5053) was also a 'Chantress of Amun'. Found together with the mummy of a man in a previously unopened courtyard tomb at Qurneh, this is a fine example. Bandaged and covered with a layer of resin which fixes it firmly to the coffin, the mummy can still be seen with its associated funerary goods, including the lotus flowers which were placed in the coffin at the time of burial.

After the third intermediate period, Egypt was ruled successively by the Greeks, under the Ptolemies, and by the Romans. Many of the funerary beliefs of the Egyptians were adopted by the conquerors, and mummification now entered its final phase. In the Ptolemaic period (332–30 BC), with the progressive decline in religious beliefs, mummification increasingly became a commercial rather than a religious concern. The outer wrappings of the mummy were elaborate and the outermost bandages were sometimes finely pleated in a series of geometrical patterns, interspersed with gilded studs. It was also customary to use three separate units of cartonnage: one piece to cover the head and shoulders; another, with representations of amulets, jewellery and religious scenes, over the chest; and a foot-piece painted to resemble a pair of sandals. Cartonnage (literally, an outer covering) was made from waste paper and sometimes included fragments of papyrus documents. Other mummies of this period display painted portrait heads on wooden panels which were placed over the face.

However, less attention was paid to the body. In some mummies, the viscera were removed, treated and returned to the body in any order; in others, the body was either filled with balls of resin- soaked linen, mud or broken pottery, or it was filled with molten resin or bitumen. In a small number of bodies, no incision was made and the viscera remained in the body.

Mummies of this period are all dark-coloured, and the skin is frequently hard and shiny. This was the result of the great reliance placed on resin as an embalming agent. In molten form, it was poured into the body cavity through the flank incision, and into the skull through the nostril or foramen magnum after brain removal; it was also applied directly to the skin surface. In many cases, however, there was no attempt to remove the brain. The body was packed with linen or mud, and sometimes resin or wax were used; the mouth and orbits were also filled with mud and linen.

It is evident that many bodies were in an advanced state of decomposition when embalming was undertaken. The molten resin frequently trapped maggots and beetles which were already feeding off the decomposing bodies, thus killing them and preserving them betwen

Fig 1.4 Painted cartonnage slippers discovered in the
bandages of Mummy 1770. The bright colours of
pink, yellow and turquoise are well preserved

Fig 1.5 Panel portrait, showing a bearded man, placed over
the face of a mummy. Graeco-Roman period (Manchester Museum)

the bandages, to be rediscovered in modern times when the mummies were unwrapped. In addition to the evidence of insect attack, x-ray evidence indicates that in some mummies partial decomposition had already set in when embalming commenced. In some cases, the head had become detached from the body, or limbs were missing, suggesting that the body had fallen apart during embalming. Some mummies present a state of utter confusion, even incorporating the bones of more than one individual. Various explanations for this have been given: with widespread mummification, which had now become a mainly commercial enterprise, there would have been a delay in starting work on the cheaper burials; also, there was undoubtedly a fall in standards of craftsmanship. However, according to Herodotus,[9] the bodies of certain women (those who had been beautiful, or had been the wives of eminent men) were not handed over to the embalmers until three or four days after death, when decomposition would have begun, presumably to inhibit necrophilia.

During the Roman period (30 BC–AD 641), mummification deteriorated still further. The mummies were simply treated to prevent decay, with the application of a thick coating of resinous substances to the surface of the body. It is not usually possible to determine whether the brain has been removed and the body eviscerated, but the outer wrappings became increasingly elaborate, and gilded head and chest covers, often inlaid with imitation jewellery, were frequently incorporated in the mummy. Towards the end of this period, during the Christian era, mummification was continued in parts of Egypt and Nubia. Although the individual likeness was no longer preserved, and evisceration was discontinued, the surface of the body was spread with natron and other substances which rendered the skin soft and pliable. Also, the body was dressed elaborately in embroidered clothes and boots, and wrapped in linen sheets. Mummification ceased to be practised altogether after the Arab invasion of Egypt in AD 641, when Islam was brought into Egypt.

The mummies in the Manchester collection include several from the Graeco-Roman period. There are three children. One, a girl (no. 1769), was discovered with the mummies of a woman and two other children at Hawara. The upper part of the body is covered with a gilded cartonnage with inlaid eyes; jewellery is also indicated on the cartonnage which is set with imitation stones. A canvas wrapper, painted with scenes of deities gilded on to a pink background, encases the lower part of the mummy, which probably dates to *c*. AD 135. The two other children (nos. 2109 and 9319), both from Hawara, provide examples of the bandagers' skills during this period. The lower parts of both mummies have elaborate diagonal bandaging, interspersed with gilt studs. No. 2109 has a cartonnage head-cover with a gilded face, and no. 9319 was originally covered with a portrait panel now in the Cairo Museum.

From the same period and site, there are three male adult mummies. One, a young man (no. 1768), has diagonal bandaging covering the lower part and a fine portrait panel over the face in which the deceased is shown wearing a laurel wreath. The second adult (no. 1767) also has a portrait panel over the face; the man is represented with a beard. The upper part of the body is covered in stucco and painted, while the lower part is encased in canvas decorated with painted deities on a red background. The third mummy (no. 1775) is covered with painted red stucco which has been brightly glazed with gum or resin; on this background, gilded figures of deities are modelled in low relief. Over the face there is one of the earliest portrait panels, showing the deceased as an elderly man, whose name, 'Artemidorus', is written across his chest. This mummy was discovered in a brick-lined chamber, together with another Artemidorus (now in the British Museum) and a lady, Thermoutharin (now in the Cairo Museum).

The three other mummies in this series are female. 'Demetria, wife of Icaious' (no. 20638) has a gilded cartonnage head and chest cover, set with imitation stones representing jewellery, and inlaid eyes; the lower part of the mummy is covered in canvas decorated with four rows of deities on a red background. The second female (no. 1766) also has a gilded cartonnage head and chest cover, again inlaid with imitation stones, and she is shown as a woman holding a bunch of red flowers. The third mummy (no. 1770) was unwrapped and investigated by the Manchester team in 1975. The general appearance of this mummy was unimpressive, but it did possess a fine cartonnage head-piece with inlaid eyes and eyebrows, which was removed and conserved.

The Manchester collection of seventeen human mummies therefore provided a fair selection of the different types of mummification for the basis of the research project, ranging from the twelfth dynasty to the Roman period, a time-span of some two thousand years.

In fact, the collection of Egyptian antiquities at the Manchester Museum is among the finest and most comprehensive in Britain. The

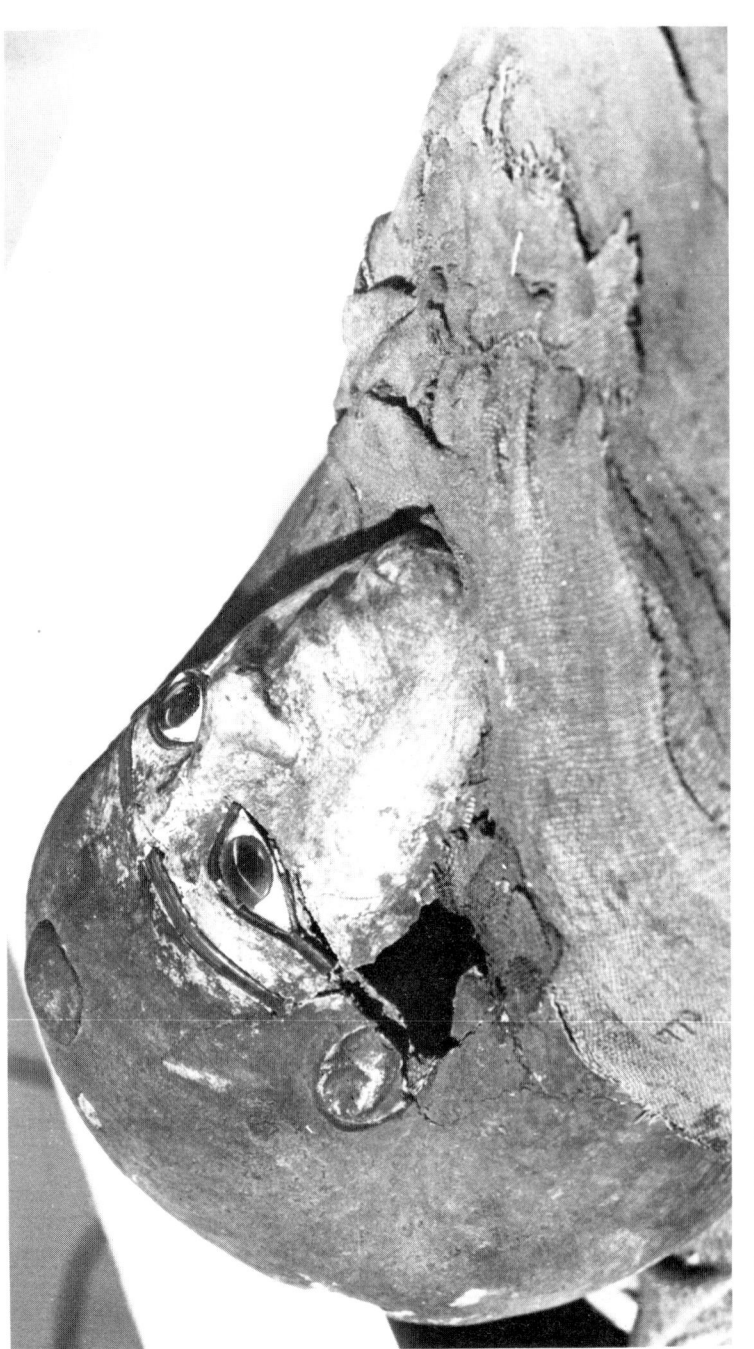

Fig 1.6 Gilded cartonnage face mask with inlaid eyes and eyebrows, belonging to Mummy 1770 (Manchester Museum)

mummies come from a number of sources and provide a good example of the variety and type of background from which many similar museum collections have been derived. Four of the mummies come directly from the excavations of the great Egyptologist, Sir William Flinders Petrie, and were added to the museum collection through the generous financial support given to several of Petrie's excavations by the Manchester businessman, Dr Jesse Haworth. Other mummies are from excavated sites in Egypt, given through the British School of Archaeology in Egypt and the Egyptian Research Account – societies founded to help and support scientific excavation in Egypt. The rationalisation of other museum collections has also benefited Manchester; one mummy was donated by the Committee of Ancoats Art Museum in Manchester, and another came from the Frewen family, via the Hastings Museum. Two mummies were received from the collection of M. E. Robinow and three others came from private donors.

Since 1979, the museum has acquired five more mummies, either as gifts or on permanent loan. These have now been subjected to intensive but non-destructive examination and have provided new information. The Phipps mummy, acquired in a sale by Miss Phipps of Westend Farm, near Stroud in Gloucestershire, came originally from the collection of Sir Percival Marling, Bt, who brought it to England in 1886 and gave it to his father. He was returning from Egypt in April 1886, granted three months' home leave, and travelled from Alexandria to Venice; in his luggage, he had '. . . a small mummy in a tin uniform case, which I has taken out of Egypt from one of the temples'. On the frontier between Italy and Switzerland, his luggage was searched by the customs officials: 'About 20 yards down the platform, I saw two gendarmes and about a dozen people and my servant in the middle fighting. I ran up to see what the row was. What had happened was this: they had opened my uniform case, and found what they thought was a corpse.' The intervention of the English vice-consul, who happened to be standing nearby, and Sir Percival's explanation in French and German regarding the true origin of the 'corpse', as well as the handing over of £5 in English gold, finally persuaded the gendarmes, one of whom Sir Percival's servant had inadvertently hit on the nose, to let them continue on their journey. The mummy was brought safely to England and stood in the ballroom of his father's house for many years.[10] This child, which is probably of the Ptolemaic period, is an interesting example of a mummy brought back from Egypt as a 'souvenir'.

A finely preserved mummy of a young child, with the remains of gilding still visible on the face and also dating to the Ptolemaic period, was given to Stonyhurst College, Lancashire, and has been placed on loan at the museum. Three other mummies on loan from Salford Museum include two wrapped mummies with wooden coffins, probably both of the third intermediate period, and the unwrapped mummy of a youth, dated to the Ptolemaic period, which came from Petrie's excavations at Hawara and was donated by Jesse Haworth; this has a fine panel portrait which remains at Salford Museum.

Historical significance of mummies

Although Egyptian mummies have long exerted a fascination for historians, paleopathologists and the general public, 'mummy' first attracted the attention of Europeans as a medicinal ingredient. As the philosopher, Sir Thomas Browne, wrote in 1658, 'Mummy is become Merchandise, Mizraim cures Wounds and Pharaoh is sold for Balsams'.

The Arab doctor and historian, Abd' el Latif, states: 'The mummy found in the hollows of corpses in Egypt differs but immaterially from the nature of mineral mummy; and where any difficulty arises in procuring the latter, may be substituted in its stead.'[11] The supposed similarity between fragments of the preserved bodies of the ancient Egyptians and the natural exudations of bituminous material from the 'Mummy Mountain' in Persia has already been noted,[12] and mummified tissue came to be credited with the same medicinal properties as natural 'mumia'.

As early as AD 1100, and probably before, doctors were prescribing mummy for their patients. Its use was established in Alexandria, and soon it was widely employed in the treatment of bruises, wounds and internal sickness. A flourishing trade emerged and, as Thomas Pettigrew in his noted monograph on Egyptian mummies states, 'No sooner was it credited that mummy constituted an article of value in the practice of medicine than many speculators embarked in the trade; the tombs were sacked, and as many mummies as could be obtained were broken into pieces for the purpose of sale.'[13]

Many foreign traders were attracted to deal in the commodity since large profits were readily attainable, and complete mummies or fragments made up into packages in Cairo and Alexandria were exported to Europe. However, the authorities in Egypt attempted to limit the exportation of mummified tissue, and demand soon exceeded supply. This led to fraudulent practises, and Guy de la Fonteine of Navarre, investigating the mummy trade in Alexandria in 1564, discovered that the bodies of the recently dead, often executed criminals, were prepared through exposure to the sun to simulate genuine mummies and the tissue was then exported as authentic 'mummy'.

In the sixteenth and seventeenth centuries, mummy had become one of the most common drugs and was sold as an expensive medicine in apothecaries' shops throughout Europe. The demand for it was apparently greatest in France, and the king, Francis I, is reputed to have always carried with him some mummy, mixed with pulverised rhubarb, for the ready treatment of his ailments. Its application was wide, for it was recommended for the treatment of abscesses, fractures, concussions, paralysis, epilepsy, coughs, nausea, ulcers and other conditions, and it was frequently mixed with other herbs for consumption by the patient.

However, although many physicians regarded it as a potent drug, one, Ambrose Paré, condemned it wholeheartedly: 'This wicked kinde of drugge, doth nothing help the diseased ... it also inferres many troublesome symptomes, as the paine of the heart or stomacke, vomiting, and stinke of the mouth.'[14]

The trade in mummies was eventually reduced when the Egyptian government began to levy substantial taxes on those dealing in the commodity, and to make it illegal to remove the mummies from Egypt. However, the trade continued, in a modified form, and the use of mummy as a medicinal ingredient continued until the early nineteenth century.

From the seventeenth century onwards, however, mummies began to attract attention as curiosities in their own right. As travellers started to visit Egypt and later, tourists took Nile trips, interest in the civilisation of ancient Egypt grew rapidly. This general enthusiasm for Egyptian curiosities encouraged museums in Europe and Britain to acquire mummies and their associated artifacts for display. One man, Giovanni Belzoni, was particularly successful in acquiring antiquities which he then sold to major museums. At Qurneh, near Luxor, wishing to obtain as many mummies as possible in as short a time as possible, he paid a regular wage and bonuses to tomb robbers. His own account of his excavations and discoveries includes a description of the physical ordeals involved in entering one tomb:

> After getting through those passages, some of them two or three hundred yards long, you generally find a more commodious place, perhaps high enough to sit. But what a place of rest: surrounded by bodies, by heaps of mummies in all directions, which, previous to my being accumstomed to the sight, impressed me with horror . . . though, fortunately, I am destitute of the sense of smelling, I could taste that the mummies were rather unpleasant to swallow.[15]

Belzoni's exhibition of some of his discoveries was opened in London on 21 May 1821, at the Egyptian Hall in Piccadilly, and continued with great success until 1822. Before the exhibition was opened to the public, an invited audience of eminent doctors watched as the mummy of a young man was unwrapped.

Other major discoveries of mummies continued to arose interest in the subject. Towards the end of the nineteenth century, the royal mummies were discovered at Deir el-Bahri, Thebes. Objects from the kings of the twenty-first dynasty began to appear on the antiquities' market, arousing suspicions that a new 'find' had been made and was being kept secret. Eventually, the discovery was revealed and the mummies were removed to the Cairo Museum. Although they included many of the mummies of the kings of the seventeenth to the twentieth dynasties, the series was incomplete, but several years later, some of these gaps were filled, when the archaeologist Loret found another cache of royal mummies in the tomb of Amenophis II at Thebes. These provided Elliot Smith with the basic material for his examination of mummification techniques.

However, although such discoveries were exciting and informative for armchair archaeologists and visitors to museums, by the second half of the nineteenth century, many travellers were spending a winter vacation in Egypt – in the words of the French archaeologist, Jean Ampère, 'a donkey-ride and a boating trip interspersed with ruins'.

Many of these visitors hired sailing boats (*dahabeeyahs*) and crews to sail up the Nile from Cairo. Some kept detailed dairies of their travels and adventures. One Victorian novelist, Amelia B. Edwards, turned her experiences into a successful book, *A Thousand Miles up the Nile*. Her visit inspired her with the desire to do something to save the monuments in Egypt, and she was instrumental in founding the Egypt Exploration Society (originally the Egypt Exploration Fund) with the aims of scientific excavation and recording the monuments. In her will, she founded and endowed the Edwards Professorship at University College London, the first chair of Egyptology in Britain. Her influence on the development of Egyptology in Britain was considerable, both in supporting archaeologists such as the young William Flinders Petrie whom she encouraged and who became the first Edwards Professor, and by inspiring interest in many non-specialists who read her book.

She describes the sights and her own feelings with clarity, and comments upon the general attitude prevailing amongst the visitors towards the acquisition of antiquities:

And then, with a shock which the present writer, at all events, will not soon forget, we suddenly discover that these scattered bones are human – that those linen shreds are shreds of cerement cloths – that yonder odd-looking brown lumps are rent fragments of what was once living flesh!... We soon become quite hardened to such sights, and learned to rummage among dusty sepulchres with no more compunction than would have befitted a gang of professional body-snatchers.[16]

Miss Edwards mentions that 'There is, in fact, a growing passion for mummies among Nile travellers'.[17] The demand, however, was so great that the prices rose accordingly, and a souvenir of a mummy became a 'costly luxury'. This eagerness to bring home a mummy is borne out in the remark made in 1833 by the monk Father Géramb to Pasha Mohammed Ali that 'It would be hardly respectable, on one's return from Egypt, to present oneself in Europe without a mummy in one hand and a crocodile in the other'.

Amelia Edwards and her companion, sailing in the 'Philae', became acquainted with two other Englishwomen, referred to as the 'M.B.s' in Miss Edwards' book. These were Miss Marianne Brocklehurst and her companion, Miss Booth, who had hired a *dahabeeyah* which they named 'Bagstones' after Miss Brocklehurst's home. Various references to the 'M.B.s' occur in Amelia Edwards' account, but an illustrated diary kept by Marianne Brocklehurst describes this journey from her own viewpoint.[18] One of the main preoccupations of this and subsequent visits to Egypt was to go 'grubbing' in the sand on visits to the various sites, for antiquities, and to supplement these by 'making bazaar' in the towns and villages along the river. Marianne Brocklehurst thus acquired a small but representative collection of Egyptian antiquities which she subsequently donated to the West Park Museum, Macclesfield, England. Her account of how she acquired a mummy and its case is of particular interest.[19] Having made approaches to the local dealers at Thebes, they sat in their *dahabeeyah*, awaiting the arrival of the mummy:

> Presently, we saw them coming down the bank carrying the horrid thing wrapped in a black cloth, all in the bright moonshine.... The Mummy was deposited in the passage where one of us stumbled over it in the dark, the bearer was thrust out of the window and all was over!

When they had removed the outer wrappings, they declared the mummy 'to be altogether a festive object and not at all a funereal old frump'. They hid the mummy in the linen closet, but finally decided to bury it 'by night with great secrecy'. However, they took the case with them, and were very relieved when the matter was finished and they had all their possessions safely on board their ship at Alexandria. The final days on the *dahabeeyah* had been particularly tense, since

> whether from the bitumen and spices with which the case was cemented inside, or what, there had been a suspicious odour in the passage near the closet when the Mummy was concealed and we feared lest the cook in particular who had been in the service of Mariette Bey[20] himself and doubtless was acquainted with the peculiar 'Mummy bouquet' might sniff him out and bring us all to grief.

Therefore, for the wealthy who collected mummies and other antiquities, Egyptology became a fashionable subject, and gradually, even European fashion, architecture and furniture were noticeably influenced by Egyptian styles and motifs. By now museums had acquired large collections, either from their support of excavations in Egypt from which sponsors received a share of the excavated material, or from private collectors who donated their treasures to the museums. In particular, mummies brought back as souvenirs eventually found their way into museum collections. The Frewen mummy (now no. 10881 in the Manchester Museum) is an interesting example of this type of transfer. Brought back from Luxor by John Frewen, the mummy stood in a glass case in the hall of Brickwall House, Northian, near Rye in Sussex for many years. However, according to Clare Sheridan, a member of the family, who recalled the mummy from childhood visits to Brickwall House, some regarded it as a sinister presence; she says: 'It was rumoured that, at the time of the mummy's arrival, the coffin case was opened, and the interior hygienically fumigated, and that as a result three servants died of an unknown disease!'[21] In 1926, when the house was turned into a school, the mummy was taken in a carrier's cart to the Hastings Museum where it was placed on loan. While it was there,

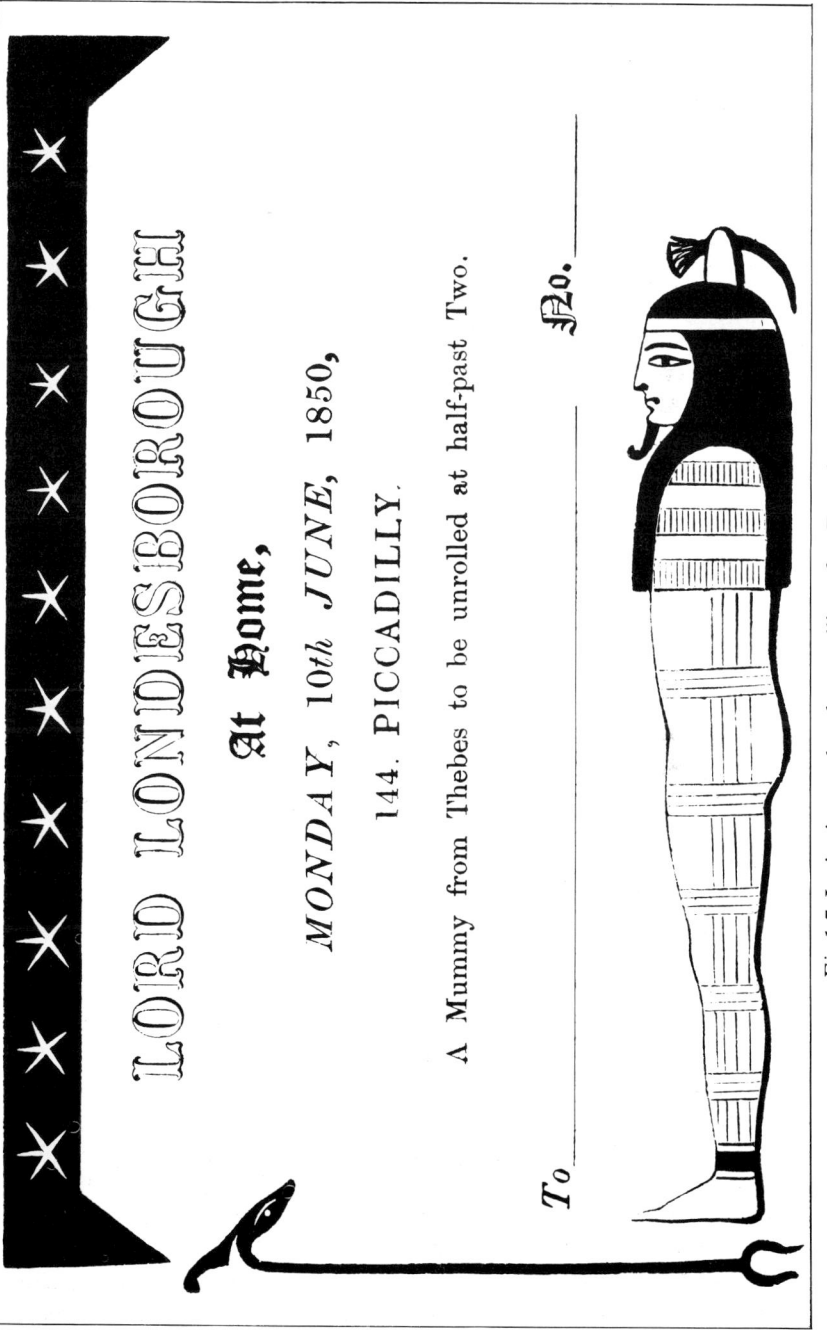

Fig 1.7 Invitation card to the unrolling of an Egyptian mummy

learned authorities examined it and declared that 'she had lived (and died) in the time of the prophet Jeremiah, a member of a middle-class family, but an heiress, and the cause of her death arthritis'. In 1947, due to reorganisation at the Hastings Museum and a decision to concentrate on local history, the mummy was offered to the Manchester Museum, where it arrived on 7 May 1948.

The unwrapping or 'unrolling' of Egyptian mummies became a not infrequent event. Some, such as the spectacle organised by Belzoni at the opening of his London exhibition in 1821, had little scientific value; others were carried out in country houses around Britain as an unusual highlight of a social evening. However, in 1834, a London surgeon, Thomas Pettigrew, published a book[22] which was later described as 'a monument of exact observation'.[23] It described the examination of a number of mummies and commented upon the development and significance of mummification. In his introduction, Pettigrew acknowledges his debt to Belzoni: 'I had the gratification of knowing the lamented Belzoni, that most intrepid and enterprising traveller, and by his kindness, I was present at the opening of three mummies.'[24] He then relates his own experiences and observations when he unrolled several mummies. Impressed by the fine quality of one mummy brought from Egypt for sale, he purchased it, and in April 1833, at Charing Cross Hospital, in front of a titled and influential audience, he unrolled it. 'This specimen', says Pettigrew,' had even been deprived of its outer roller and bandages; but the dry state of those that remained, together with the evidences of their being genuine, induced me to become the purchaser of the mummy, and to be sanguine as to the result of its examination.' Other mummies purchased by Pettigrew or presented to him for this purpose by friends and colleagues were subsequently unrolled and investigated at various London venues, in front of titled, medical, literary and scientific audiences. Fairly detailed accounts are given of the procedure adopted at each unwrapping and experts were consulted regarding aspects of the examination, such as the textile fibre of the bandages and the identification of insects found in the mummies. Pettigrew placed the examination of mummies on a scientific basis and laid the foundation for future research; the unwrapping of a mummy was no longer a frivolous pursuit.

In the early years of the twentieth century, the work of three men in Cairo further advanced Egyptian paleopathology. Grafton Elliot Smith, Armand Ruffer and Alfred Lucas were respectively professors of anatomy, bacteriology and chemistry at the Government School of Medicine in Cairo. Elliot Smith's early work involved a series of studies carried out on Egyptian bodies in Upper Egypt in 1901, in which the bone measurements were taken and the mummification procedures were examined. The discovery of the tomb of King Tuthmosis IV in 1903 was followed by a public unwrapping and examination of the mummy in Cairo, but the detailed private investigation later carried out by Elliot Smith was more significant and included the first use of roentgenography for the study of a royal mummy. Since there was only one x-ray machine in Cairo, Elliot Smith and Howard Carter were obliged to transfer the rigid mummy of the king to the nursing home in a taxi-cab.

Elliot Smith also carried out an extensive study of the royal mummies found in the two caches at Deir el-Bahri, Thebes, and was able to utilise the information gained from this to compile a history of the development of the techniques used in mummification. This provided the basis for two classic works on Egyptian mummies.[25]

From 1900 onwards, alterations were carried out on the dam at Aswan in Upper Egypt, with the result that many mummies were destroyed by the rising water levels. Elliot Smith headed a rescue operation in which hurried investigations were carried out on thousands of mummies. Autopsies performed on some six thousand mummies revealed for the first time many of the diseases from which the ancient Egyptians had suffered. So enormous was this task that two other specialists, W. R. Dawson and F. Wood Jones, were sent from England to assist with the project.

The work of the other two pioneers was equally significant. Armand Ruffer laid the foundations for the study of histopathology in relation to Egyptian mummified remains. He experimented successfully with methods of restoring ancient tissues by means of rehydration so that the tissues resumed something of their original condition prior to death. Histological examination of the rehydrated tissue then enabled him to determine disease in some of the mummies. His work continues to provide the basis for the advanced studies of the present day. Alfred Lucas' contribution is presented in his book – an account of his analysis of the materials used by the ancient Egyptians.[26] His experiments in relation to techniques of mummification were the first to show that much of Herodotus' account was accurate but that the bodies were almost certainly packed with dry natron and not immersed in a natron solution. He also played a significant part in the initial investigation of the mummy of Tutankhamun.

In England, in the meantime, an important multi-disciplinary un-wrapping and investigation of two mummies was held in Manchester in 1908. In 1877, Jesse Haworth, a local textile merchant, had read Amelia Edwards' *A Thousand Miles up the Nile* and took his wife on a similar visit to Egypt. This kindled his enthusiasm for Egyptology, and the Haworths subsequently became friends of Miss Edwards. In 1887, she readily persuaded Jesse Haworth to provide financial assistance for excavation in Egypt. He and another patron, Martyn Kennard, agreed to wholly support the excavations of the brilliant young Egyptologist, William Flinders Petrie, at the sites of Kahun, Illahun and Gurob. Petrie met his own expenses, but his benefactors paid for the local workmen and transport, and the antiquities found at the sites were divided equally amongst them when they were brought back to England. In 1890, the two patrons presented their valuable collection from these sites to the Manchester Museum, and thus formed the nucleus of one of the best Egyptology collections in Britain.

The results of Petrie's work aroused public interest all over the country; excavation societies, such as the British School of Archaeology in Egypt, were founded, whose members subscribed to support his work. Public institutions and private individuals who funded the excavations in this way received divisions of the finds in proportion to the local contribution. Jesse Haworth's continuing beneficence thus ensured that objects of the finest quality entered the Manchester collection, and in 1906, when Petrie addressed an enthusiastic audience in Manchester, on the subject of setting up a local society, the Manchester Egyptian Association was founded, with Jesse Haworth as its first president.

The society flourished for many years and attracted a notable membership, and Manchester rapidly became a centre of Egyptological studies. In 1909, Elliot Smith, who was professor of anatomy at Manchester, became a member of the association, and in 1910 he delivered a lecture on the 'royal mummies' before a large audience. Petrie also continued to provide a stimulus for the subject by returning every year to deliver the first Museum Lecture of the session.

By 1911, it had become necesary to provide suitable accommodation within the museum (which was a university department) for the rapidly growing Egyptian collection. The university considered the scheme and the Egyptian Association opened a public fund, but it was again Jesse Haworth's generosity which finally enabled the scheme to be carried out. In recognition of this, and of his position as one of the first patrons of scientific excavation in Egypt, the University of Machester awarded him the degree of Doctor of Laws in 1912.

The first curator of this outstanding Egyptian collection was one of Petrie's pupils, Dr Margaret Murray, and it was she who, on 6 May 1908, unwrapped the mummies of the Two Brothers and directed the first major multi-disciplinary investigation of mummified remains. The unwrapping ceremony took place in the chemistry theatre of the university and was held instead of one of the usual meetings of the Egyptian Association; the audience was composed of invited members of the association and other friends of the museum. Margaret Murray conducted the unwrapping, with the assistance of Mr Standen, Mr Wilfred Jackson, Miss Wilkinson and Miss Hart-Davis. One of the Two Brothers – Khnum-Nakht – was unwrapped publicly before the audience of five hundred people. The procedure lasted one and a half hours, but the audience were rewarded for their patience, for 'at the close of the ceremony, members . . . who wished to have a piece of the mummy wrappings as a memento were invited by the Chairman to leave their names and addresses'.

This public ceremony, however, was only the start of an intensive and multi-disciplinary survey of the two mummies and their associated tomb goods, the full account being published in 1910 by Margaret Murray.[27] The tomb-group, discovered in a twelfth dynasty rock-tomb at Rifeh, some eight miles south of Assiut in Middle Egypt,[28] was purchased for the Manchester collection by public subscription. Petrie wrote in 1907 to give details of this discovery and to report that, if Manchester could contribute £500 to the future excavations at Memphis, the Committee would allot it the complete tomb-group. The sum of £570.19s was quickly raised, and not only was the tomb-group acquired but the additional sum was used to produce Margaret Murray's *Memoir* on the scientific investigation of the mummies.

In her introduction to this, she refutes the arguments of those who would criticise the new scientific approach:

Archaeology has been raised to the rank of a science within one generation: before that it was merely the pastime of the dilettante and the amateur who amused himself by adding beautiful specimens to his collection of ancient art. . . . Then came the period of the enthusiast in languages, to whom

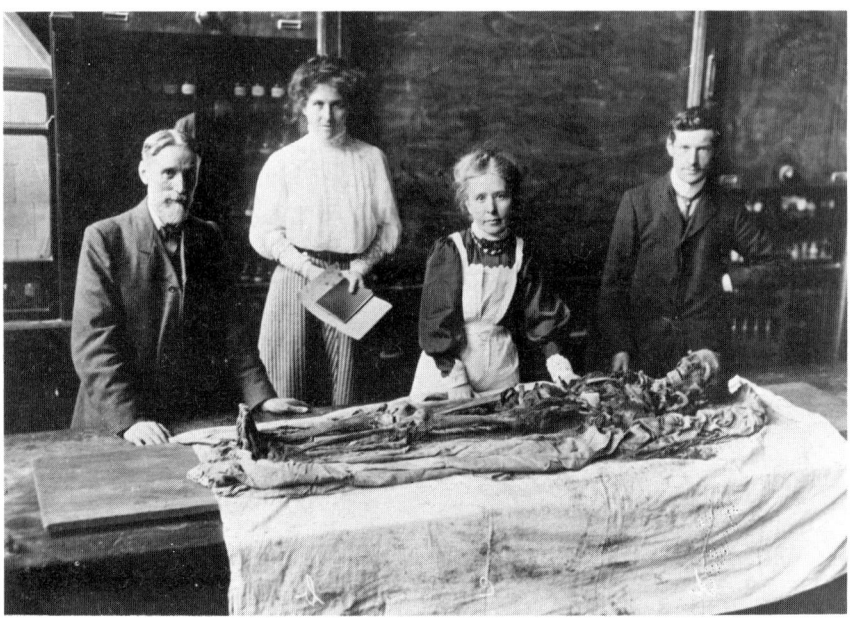

Fig 1.8 Dr Margaret Murray and colleagues at the unwrapping
of the Two Brothers in Manchester

Fig 1.9 Model boat from the tomb of the Two Brothers at Rifeh
(Manchester Museum)

inscriptions were the joy of life. And now there has arisen a new school to whom archaeology is a science, a science which embraces the whole field of human activity.[29]

It is only by opening graves and by examining their contents, she claims, that new knowledge can be gained: ' . . . every vestige of ancient remains must be carefully studied and recorded without sentimentality and without fear of the outcry of the ignorant.' And she further supports her argument by quoting from Petrie:

To raid the whole of past ages, and put all that we think effective into museums is only to ensure that such things will perish in course of time. A museum is only a temporary place. There is not one storehouse in the world that has lasted a couple of thousand years. . . . It is then to the written record and the published illustrations that the future will have mainly to look.[30]

Her published account of this investigation is a good example of how multi-disciplinary research can provide as near a complete picture as possible of the history and background of the human remains and artifacts. It represents a major step forward in this type of approach.

The tomb at Rifeh – large, unsculptured and hewn from the rock – was filled completely with funerary equipment. The burial included the mummies of Khnum-Nakht and Nekht-Ankh and their tomb goods. The mummies were each placed inside a body coffin, enclosed in a rectangular coffin. A wooden chest contained the mummified viscera of Nekht-Ankh. There were two model boats, to travel upstream and downstream on the Nile after death, figurines of offering-bearers, pottery vessels and statuettes of the brothers. The wood from which the coffins were made was examined by a botanist and identified as *Ficus sycomorus,* while the coffin pegs were of acacia wood; leaves and stalks found in the pottery vessels were identified as a species of laurel.

The mummies and their wrappings were subjected to the most intensive scrutiny. It was quite evident that two different techniques of mummification had been used for the bodies. The mummy of Nekht-Ankh, in a poor state of preservation before unwrapping, had dark brown skin which was in a state of almost perfect preservation on the face and was generally quite moist. Hair remained on the head and sides of the face, and the chest cavity was packed with matting. Many beetles were found in the innermost bandages but not on the outer ones, indicating that they had bred under the folds of the linen. The beetles were identified as *Gibbium scotias.* The set of canopic jars and their contents belonged to Nekht-Ankh, and the viscera were partially identified by Dr J. Cameron.

By contrast, the mummy of Khnum-Nakht was completely dry, and the tissues resolved into dry powder when the mummy was handled; where it remained, the skin was white. There were no insect remains, and no canopic jars had been provided for this man.

Dr Cameron also carried out a detailed anatomical examination of the skeletal remains of the brothers. Most remarkable were the distinct racial differences evidenced in the two skeletons; Khnum-Nakht possessed a markedly prognathous or negroid type of skull, while the other was orthognathous. Also, there was some indication in the skeleton of Nekht-Ankh that he may have been a eunuch. The coffin inscriptions provide the name of the mother but not of the father and, together with the skeletal evidence, this has led to the suggestion that they may have been half-brothers; it is also possible, however, that one was an adopted son, a practice not uncommon in ancient Egypt.

Chemical analysis of the inorganic constituents of the mummies, carried out by another scientist, showed that two very different techniques of mummification were used. A detailed study was also made of the bandages – of their position and order upon the body, and of the types of linen of which the bandages and cloths were made, as well as an analysis of the colouring matter with which they had been dyed.

During the current project, the Two Brothers have again been subjected to intensive study, and it has been possible to add further information to the earlier results. Further anatomical studies have lent support to the original findings, and histological investigation of lung tissue from one of the canopic jars has shown that Nekht-Ankh suffered from diseases which affected the lungs and the heart. These included sand pneumoconiosis, inflammation of the surface of the lung (pleurisy) and of the heart (pericarditis). Electron microscopy was also used to identify other insect remains; the predominant beetle was an unusual species, *Gibbium psylloides* (the hump-spider beetle), and smaller numbers of another beetle, *Mesostenopa*, also occurred. The data from the dental and anatomical studies provided the basis for the remarkable, scientifically reconstructed, three-dimensional heads of the Two Brothers; these, in turn, laid the groundwork for the more exacting reconstruction of the head of 1770.

The continuing study of mummies has gained momentum in recent years. In addition to the new investigation of the mummies of Tutankhamun and Smenkhkare in the 1960s, a radiological study of the royal mummies in the Cairo Museum has been carried out by J. E. Harris, E. F. Wente and their colleagues.[31] A joint American and Canadian project has surveyed mummified remains not only from Egypt but from many other parts of the world.[32] This has included performing autopsies on various Egyptian mummies, including a series from the Pennsylvania University Museum, Philadelphia, and from the Royal Ontario Museum in Canada. The autopsy carried out on PUM II (the second mummy in the series from Philadelphia) in 1973, at the Wayne State University Medical School, Detroit, Michigan, revealed a good example of the classic, expensive method of mummification, while those performed on the mummies known as PUM III and PUM IV provided evidence of the cheaper techniques, with evisceration *per anum*. The multi-disciplinary nature of these investigations has added much to existing knowledge of paleopathology.

However, in Manchester, when in 1975 the first scientific unwrapping of an Egyptian mummy took place in Britain after seventy years, the team had an opportunity to involve as many disciplines and techniques as were available to them, and, ultimately, to consider methods which, in the future, would provide virtually non-destructive means of obtaining the required data. The selection of a mummy for unwrapping and autopsy was governed by various factors. Mummy 1770 had no elaborate decorative bandaging and was unsuitable for display purposes in the museum; also, preliminary x-rays had shown that the lower parts of the legs were missing and that an unidentifiable object lay close to the ends of the leg bones. After a further, complete radiological survey of the mummy, and completion of all the preparations, the unwrapping was carried out in the Medical School of the University of Manchester over a period of two weeks. A detailed record was kept of the procedure, using both still and ciné photography; every fragment of bone, tissue and bandage was preserved, numbered and registered.

In the course of the unwrapping, samples of the bandages were removed at different levels for further examination. A complete study was also made of the insect remains retrieved from the bandages. The artifacts found within the mummy included a fine gilded cartonnage head-mask, a cartonnage chest cover and painted slippers; gilded finger- and toe-nail covers had been placed on the mummy, and

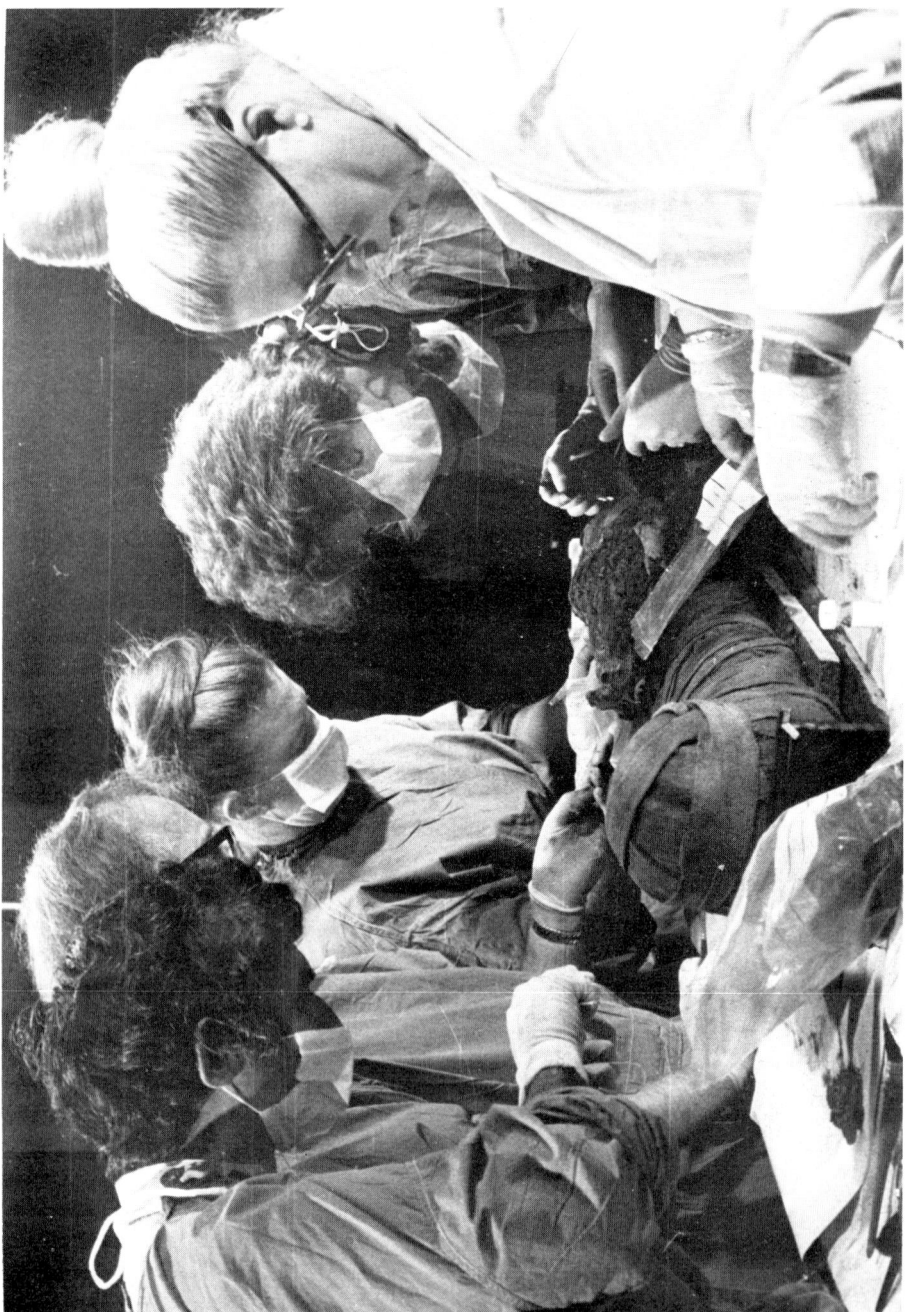

Fig 1.10 (opposite) Members of the Manchester Mummy Research Team
at the unwrapping of Mummy 1770 in the Medical School,
University of Manchester, June 1975

Fig 1.11 Legs of Mummy 1770, revealed during the unwrapping,
showing amputations and prosthetic limbs inserted alongside the bones

prosthetic legs were present to replace the missing lower limbs. The body, in a poor state of preservation, had very little recognisable skin, muscle or soft tissue; the bones of the neck and skull were fragmented and could be removed piecemeal. However, the bones forming the upper jaw and face were intact. The abdomen and pelvis were packed with bandages and mud, and the bones of the pelvis were broken; a careful search of this packing failed to show any sign of the viscera. However, a hard mass, one inch in diameter, was found in the abdominal wall, and this proved to be the calcified remains of a parasite, Guinea-worm. The unwrapping of the legs revealed that the limbs had been amputated, the left leg below the knee, through the tibia, and the right above the knee, through the femur. Artificial limbs, made of wood, were splinted to the bone and covered with mud. The unidentified object seen in this area in the preliminary x-rays was now revealed as a pair of false feet. The right one was an intricate structure of reeds and mud with the ends of the reeds forming toes, but the left 'foot' consisted simply of an irregular mass of mud and reeds. Gilded toe-nail covers, similar to those found in position on the fingers, had been provided for the 'feet' and were placed between the foot bandages. The fine pair of cartonnage slippers was also included for use in the afterlife.

The information obtained from the autopsy gave rise to much speculation. The poor health of the girl was evident from several factors, including the presence of the Guinea-worm remains which indicated disease, and the fact that there is little evidence of wearing away of the surface of the teeth, which probably suggests that she was on a semi-liquid or invalid diet for much of her short life. Examination of the irregular amputation lines on her legs and the fact that there is no bony callus on the ends of the femur have indicated that the fracture probably occurred round about the time of death, or even a week or two before. However, the reason for the amputation has presented a problem and remains a matter for speculation.

Perhaps the most intriguing mystery centred around the sex and identity of the mummy. The embalmers, preparing the body in the Graeco-Roman period, included not only gold nipple covers – amulets to ensure lactation in female mummies in the afterlife – but also a roll of bandages in the form of a false phallus, which was usually supplied for a male mummy. Despite the fairly elaborate preparations of the body, it is evident that the embalmers were uncertain of the sex and, therefore, of the identity of this person. Speculation about the reason for this apparent inconsistency continued after the unwrapping was completed. A plausible theory was that, since the body was in an advanced state of decomposition when it was prepared and since the embalmers were seemingly ignorant of its identity, perhaps this was the body of an unknown person which had been found in the Nile, partly devoured by crocodiles. Further support was given to this theory by the passage in an ancient writer where it is explained that, since such bodies were particularly sacred, it was the duty of the local authority to provide an elaborate burial for them.

However, the results of the carbon-14 dating of the bones and bandages of 1770 suggested another reason to explain some of the inconsistencies. The bandages were shown to date to the Graeco-Roman period of Egypt's history, while the bones were of an earlier date, indicating that the body predated the wrappings by some eight hundred years. The body was apparently rewrapped, with the associated decorations and artifacts, in the later period, by the embalmers who were uncertain of its identity. We can only speculate that perhaps the find-spot of this body may have led to the conclusion that this was a person of some significance who warranted an elaborate restoration and rewrapping to ensure continuation in the afterlife.

The identity of 1770 will never be known, but modern studies have shown that this is the mummy of a female, aged about fourteen years at death; a girl who suffered poor health for most of her life. In the scientific reconstruction of her face, however, we can gain a realistic impression of her appearance in life.

It can be argued that autopsies on mummies deplete the already limited number of available specimens. However, by investigating one mummy in this way, it was possible to apply a whole range of techniques to the examination of the human remains, and some facts were discovered which, at that time, could not have been revealed by any less destructive method of examination. Nevertheless, there is much to be said in favour of the argument that the unwrapping and autopsy of a mummy should be a rare event and should only be undertaken if new and significant information is likely to be obtained.

The Manchester team decided that the future aim of their work should be the development of a set of techniques which would be totally or virtually non-destructive, but which would provide the paleopathologist with the maximum information. Such development would make it possible to continue to add to existing knowledge on disease and living conditions in ancient Egypt, without the need to perform any more autopsies. With this objective, and with the aim of augmenting their existing methods of examination, the Manchester team spent the years from 1979 to 1983 developing the project along these lines. The following chapters tell this story.

⟦Part II⟧
THE INVESTIGATION

[[2]]

X-RAYING THE
MANCHESTER MUMMIES

Since radiography is a non-destructive scientific method of examination which can yield much accurate information, it was the first technique applied in the investigation of the human and animal mummies in the Manchester Museum collection. Since 1973, these have been the subject of radiological survey and the results have added considerable information to the overall study of the mummies.

Despite its obvious advantages, however, radiography had not been extensively used in this field until recent years. Its possibilities were initially realised after the discovery of x-rays by Roentgen in 1895, some objects were thus recorded in the nineteenth century.[1] These included a human mummy which Flinders Petrie examined radiologically in Cairo in 1898.[2] Elliot Smith and Howard Carter x-rayed the mummy of Tuthmosis IV in 1904,[3] but it was not until 1931 that Moodie carried out one of the first comprehensive studies of a collection of mummies in Chicago.[4] More recently, since 1960, a series of systematic radiological surveys of collections in European institutions has been conducted by Gray.[5] In the early days, exposure times had to be long and this was a limiting factor in the medical field, but at least movement never presented any difficulties in the study of Egyptian mummies!

The current survey has been carried out under near-ideal conditions. Previously, most of the recorded radiographic work on mummified remains had to be undertaken in museums or at archaeological sites, using portable x-ray equipment and with the inevitable limitations of local electrical supplies and processing facilities. Poorly controlled film processing and reproducibility frequently led to less than optimum results and inadequate scientific data. However, the Manchester Museum, as a university institution, is well-placed to enlist the aid of a number of medical and scientific colleagues from the Manchester

Medical School and the Royal Infirmary and to permit the temporary removal of the mummified remains to the neuroradiology department of the hospital for examination. Here, complex specialised equipment used in advanced medical radiological investigations has provided detailed information which would otherwise have been unobtainable.[6] The studies have been carried out at weekends and in off-duty periods, in order not to interfere with the normal work of a busy department, nor to encounter unwary patients. The hospital authorities granted permission to use the equipment and the premises, and supplies of x-ray film were donated by Kodak Ltd, specifically for this survey.

Radiographic equipment and techniques

Significant advances in x-ray apparatus, methods of image display, and in medical radio-diagnois have been made in the last eight years, but the basic principles of x-ray production and transmission have not changed. These can be summarised as follows. X-ray energy photons are transmitted by matter to a greater or lesser degree, depending on three factors. These are the atomic number of the components of the material through which x-ray photons pass; the electron density; and the energy of the x-ray beam. The higher the atomic number or the greater the electron density, the greater the absorption at diagnostic x-ray energies. A suitable detector system – in its simplest form, a special photographic film – can be used to measure the transmitted x-rays. The degree of film blackening represents the absorption characteristic of the material under investigation.

Alternatively, the transmitted photons can be converted into light photons using a suitable light emitting phosphor. This can then be photographed by direct contact using a film in a holder or cassette, or the light can be intensified by electronic and geometric means. The intensified light image can then be photographed by a 'spot' camera or a television camera, and the information recorded retrospectively on film or in real time on a television monitor. Video recording of the television image is also possible. The term used for such film recording of the image is photofluorography.

The specialised equipment used for this purpose consists of an x-ray source and imaging system, mounted on a U-shaped arm in such a way that the imaging system can orbit the x-ray couch on which the subject rests. The part under examination is placed at the centre of an imaginary sphere and viewed by the imaging system from suitable vantage points at the surface of that sphere. This type of equipment enables the subject to be viewed from any chosen angle. The imaging system is simply moved around the subject, whose position need not be altered. It is often necessary to obtain multiple angles of view to reveal detailed anatomy which is concealed by superimposed structures.

Tomography (sectional radiography) is another technique available for investigation. It enables a single layer of tissue to be isolated from its background and represented relatively sharply as a focal plane against the blurred layers lying above and beneath it. To achieve this, the x-ray source and film are made to move synchronously and equally in opposite directions. At the level of the pivot or fulcrum, no movement takes place and structures in this plane are thus rendered sharply in the resultant image. The greater the angle of the imaging system movement, the thinner the layer of material 'in focus'. Tomography is particularly useful in the examination of wrapped mummies, where it enables parts of the body to be seen which would otherwise be obscured by coverings or by superimposed bony structures.

A new and even more complex radiological system, recently installed in the neuroradiology department, has made it easier to obtain a three dimensional 'view' of the subject. The imaging system is moved in a chosen orbit around the subject and the image is viewed in a 'continuous' way on a television monitor as the orbiting manoeuvre is being carried out. This technique has been of considerable assistance in the recent endoscopic examinations of some of the body or head cavities in the mummies. Small biopsy specimens of selected tissue have been removed from the interior of the body or the head for rehydration and analytical examination. It has been possible to use the imaging technique not only to obtain three dimensional guidance for manoeuvring the endoscope, but also to record the biopsy site, using a 105 mm camera in conjunction with the image intensifier (photofluography). Radiographs were thus obtained in at least two dimensions.

Various radiographic techniques have been used in examining the mummies, and a protocol has been established.[7] This commences with an 'over view', and the fluoroscopic technique is used to determine first the presence of a body within the wrappings, and then, the disposition of the remains. The anatomical levels and planes are marked with tape on the outer mummy case, for future reference.

An initial set of radiographs are prepared, from which the subsequent examination can be planned. These consist of a series of large, over-lapping radiographs, obtained in the antero-posterior and lateral planes; to limit geometric magnification and to present as near true measurements as possible in the radiographs, a long source/film distance (180 cms) is selected. The head is given special attention, and both standard skull projections and tomograms are taken to search for a possible site of brain removal, as well as prostheses such as artificial eyes, and brain tissue remnants, damage prior to death, or any other pathological defects. The dental state is also assessed and the teeth on either side of the jaw are radiographed separately, using thick suitably angled tomographic sections. Similar tomographs are made of the incisor teeth.

Tomography is also used to search the thorax (chest) and abdomen for remnants of organs or for mummified, packaged organs which have been re-inserted there. Items of jewellery designed to provide magical protection (often referred to as 'amulets') were frequently inserted between the bandages, and if these have been noted on the 'over view', tomography is used to supply further information. Finally, the skeleton is examined for evidence of disease or injury which may give some clue concerning the cause of death.

In child mummies, it is particularly important to discover the age at death. Thus, apart from dental ageing, we need information about bone age, and attention is paid to hand and wrist, elbow, shoulder, hip and knee joints, so that bone ossification and growth plate fusion can be displayed. This is then compared with known appearances used for current bone age assessment. However, there are problems with this method, for bone maturity in ancient Egyptians must have differed from current standards, and these modern standards may also reflect different racial and genetic influences.

In the human mummies, it is initially necessary to determine the presence of a body within the wrappings. With the animal mummies, in addition, the animal species must be radiologically determined, since the outer wrappings and representations do not inevitably signify the nature of the contents.

Radiological analysis

In the following survey, each mummy has been identified by the name or number provided by the Manchester Museum. Using the established protocol, the radiographs of each mummy have been reviewed in detail, thus enabling a comparable assessment to be made and detailed features to be recorded. The following reports refer exclusively to the radiological appearances.

Salford head

General observations A complete skull, disarticulated at the skull base, but otherwise in a good state of preservation.

Skull The skull vault is intact and there is no bony damage to indicate a site of brain removal. There is no evidence of dural remains or resin within the cranial vault, but in the posterior part of the cranial cavity there is a dense mass with an irregular anterior margin. This shows a central vertical fissure on the frontal view and the appearances suggest the presence of brain tissue. Irregular curvilinear shadows are seen within the right bony orbit which may well be within packing material. The nasal cavity is completely empty and the nasal septum is intact. The pituitary fossa, petrous bones, mastoids and sutures are all normal.

Dental state The right upper first and second pre-molar teeth have erupted but the canines and remaining pre-molars are present but unerupted. These appearances would indicate a dental age of approximately eleven years.

Comments An extremely well-preserved detached head of a young person of around eleven years age at death. The contents of the skull do not have the layered configuration normally associated with resin and thus are presumed to be preserved brain tissue with both cerebral hemispheres and cerebellum visible.

Head 214575

General observations A whole head disarticulated at mid-cervical spine level and in a moderate state of preservation.

Skull The skull vault is intact. Damage to the ethmoidal sinus anteriorly and the anterior nasal septum indicates that the brain was removed via the nose. The left anterior clinoid process is missing and this damage presumably occurred during the process of brain removal. There is no evidence of dural remains but a thin occipital fluid level indicates the presence of resin in the cranial cavity. An irregular margin between the resin and the foramen magnum may represent a small amount of residual brain tissue. The eye sockets show definite evidence

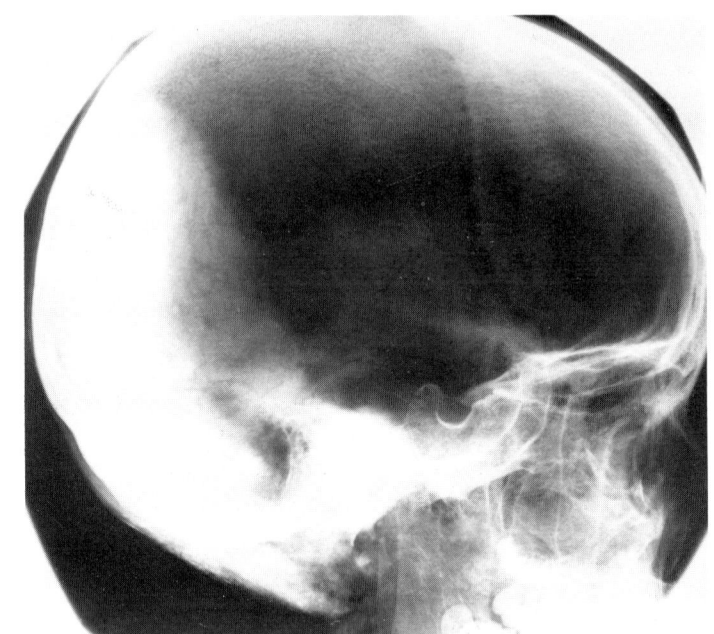

2.1

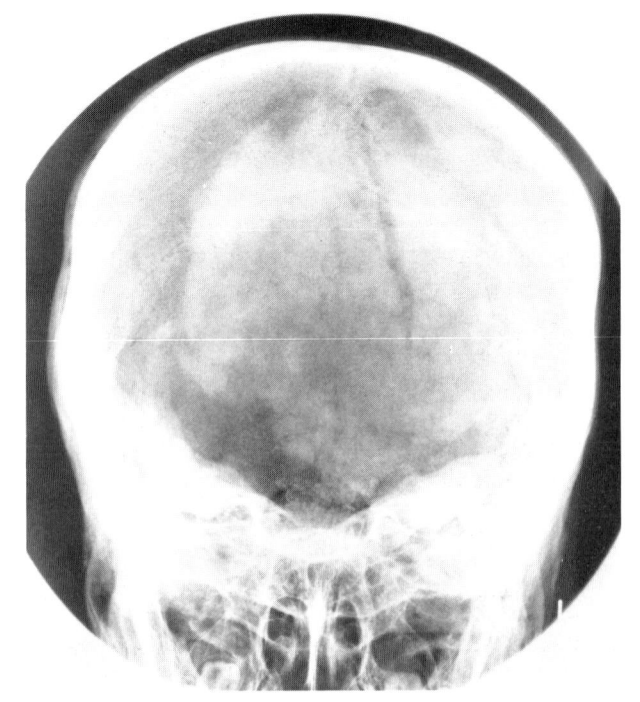

2.2

of packing with what appears to be mud. Packing is also seen posteriorly in the nasopharynx.

Dental state The general dental condition is poor with widespread attrition. There is a clean empty tooth socket and a loose molar tooth is seen in the tissues of the left sub-mandibular region which would imply dislodgement of this tooth after death. Peri-apical disease is present at lower jaw (right), no. 4 and upper jaw (right and left), no. 1.

Comment A moderately preserved adult human head which has been disarticulated at mid cervical level. The teeth show general attrition which has been previously reported in ancient Egyptian mummies.[8] Evidence of *post mortem* brain tissue removal and resin in the cranial cavity is also in keeping with previous findings. The insertion of the linen pack into the back of the mouth may have dislodged the molar tooth.

Head 1981/575

General observations A whole head with a face mask, in a good state of preservation but disarticulated at the skull base.

Skull The skull vault is intact but there is anterior fossa damage with destruction of the cribiform plate, indicating the site of brain removal. Dural remains are visible in the right parasellar region. A distinct single fluid level of resin which shows some unusual fissuring is clearly seen in the occipital region. The eye sockets appear to contain globes bilaterally and there is a suggestion of the lens within the right globe. A facial profile is just visible in the region of the mouth.

Dental state The state of the teeth is excellent. All permanant teeth are present and in good condition although there is early attrition of all four first molar teeth.

Comment This is a visually attractive wrapped head in a good state of preservation. There is clear evidence of *post mortem* brain removal and the intracranial resin shows the unusual fissuring. The good dental state with only limited and early attrition would indicate that the skull is that of a young adult.

Fig 2.1 Salford Head – the lateral view shows brain residue

Fig 2.2 Salford Head – the occipital view shows an almost vertical fissure, presumably between the cerebral hemispheres

Stonyhurst mummy

General observations   This complete body, which measures 97.5 cms from the crown of the head to the heels, lies outstrectched with the head turned towards the right. The arms are stretched out by the sides with the hands resting against the outer thighs. The body is in an excellent state of preservation with no signs of disturbance after mummification. There are no radio-opaque amulets present.

Skull   The cranial bones are intact and there is no bone damage to indicate the site of brain removal. Part of the dura mater lies obliquely in the coronal plane across the cranial cavity. There is no intracranial fluid level but crescentic layering with an upper irregular margin is present in the occipital region, suggesting a possible combination of resin and brain tissue. The eye sockets contain probable globes and a dense artifact is present in the supero-lateral quadrant of the right orbit, lying outside the globe. The nasal cavity is intact and devoid of any packing. The spheno-occipital synchondrosis is seen – normal finding in a young child.

Dental state   The deciduous dentition is complete, with no evidence of dental disease. No secondary teeth have as yet erupted although the permanent first molar teeth are in the course of eruption. This suggests a dental age of around five years.

Limbs   The bony skeleton of all four limbs shows no abnormality but the speckled opacities in the overlying soft tissues, noted in previous work, are seen in this mummy. Cartilage in the joint spaces is opacified. The state of bone epiphyses and the appearances of the hand and wrist on tomography would indicate a bone age of five to six years.

Thorax   The bony thorax is complete and undisturbed. Some residual mediastinal structures are seen to the left of the midline but no specific organs can be identified by tomography.

Abdomen and pelvis   No incision site or incision plate is visible nor is there any evidence of packaging. There are however some organ remnants contained within the pelvic cavity and male genitalia are present.

Spine   All vertebrae are present and normal. The intervertebral spaces are well preserved and there is opacification of the intervertebral disc material.

Comment   This mummy of a five to six year old boy is in an excellent state of preservation. There is an unusual display of dural remains in the cranial cavity. The absence of Harris lines, lines of temporarily arrested growth, indicate a healthy childhood and no cause of death has been demonstrated radiologically. This child mummy presents a good example of the use of dental development as a guide to the age at death.

Phipps mummy

General observations   The body measures 81 cms from the crown of the head to the heels. It lies supine with the head slightly turned. The arms are extended with the left hand over the left groin and the right hand against the lateral aspect of the right thigh. The mummy is well preserved and shows no evidence of disturbance.

Skull   The cranium is intact and there is no bony evidence of brain removal. A small amount of dura appears attached to the floor of the anterior fossa and there is bridging of the sella turcica, but no intracranial resin is seen. The left bony orbit contains an irregular shaped density and there is speckling in the right orbit, but no clear outline of a globe can be identified. The nasal cavity is intact and the nasal septum bows towards the left. On close scrutiny, the facial profile is just visible.

Dental state   All the deciduous teeth are present and erupted, a feature which would point to a dental age of over two years. There is no evidence of any dental disease.

Limbs   All four limbs are intact but there are none of the speckled densities sometimes seen in the soft tissues. Harris lines are present towards the ends of both upper and lower limbs. Of the epiphyses in the hands, the base of the first metacarpal is present and the bases of the middle phalanges just visible. These features indicate a bone age of just under three years.

Thorax   The bony thorax is complete and intact and the diaphragm is clearly visible, with upper and middle mediastinal residue revealed on tomography. Fissured resin is seen in the right lower thorax, lying against the posterior wall.

Abdomen and pelvis   The outline of either liver or kidney can be seen lying in the right upper quadrant of the abdomen. There is a suggestion of male genitalia being present.

Spine   The spine is complete, with the noteworthy feature being the opacification of intervertebral disc material.

Comment   This is the well preserved mummy of a young child probably male, who was about three years old at the time of death. The

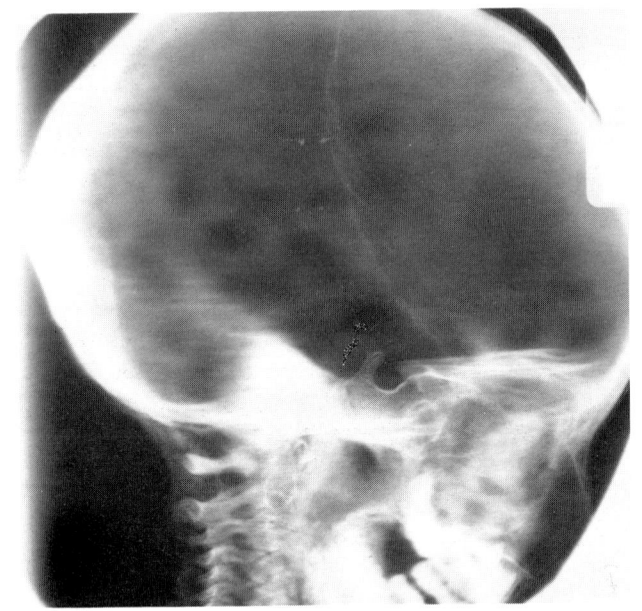

2.3

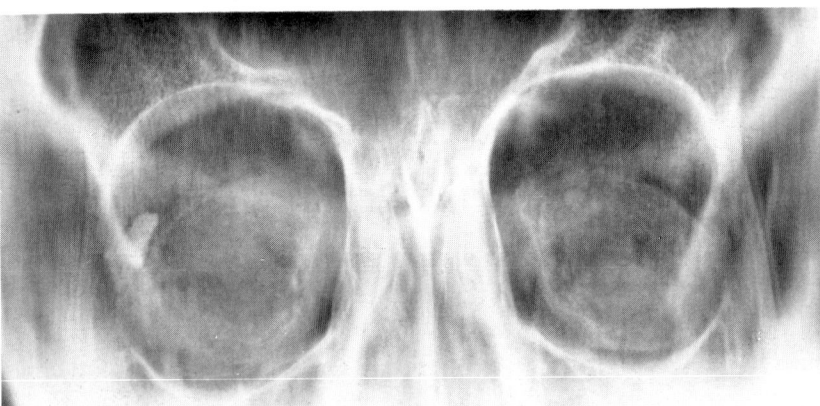

2.4

Fig 2.3 Stonyhurst mummy – midline tomography of skull showing a thin
line of dura mater across the skull cavity and a crescent-shaped
rim of resin at the back of the head

Fig 2.4 Stonyhurst mummy – anteroposterior tomography shows eyeballs
within both sockets, together with a small dense opacity on the right

Fig 2.5 Stonyhurst mummy – lateral tomography confirms the spheres,
presumed to be eyeballs

Fig 2.6 Stonyhurst mummy – tomography shows dental development.
The first premolar is about to erupt, allowing an accurate assessment of age

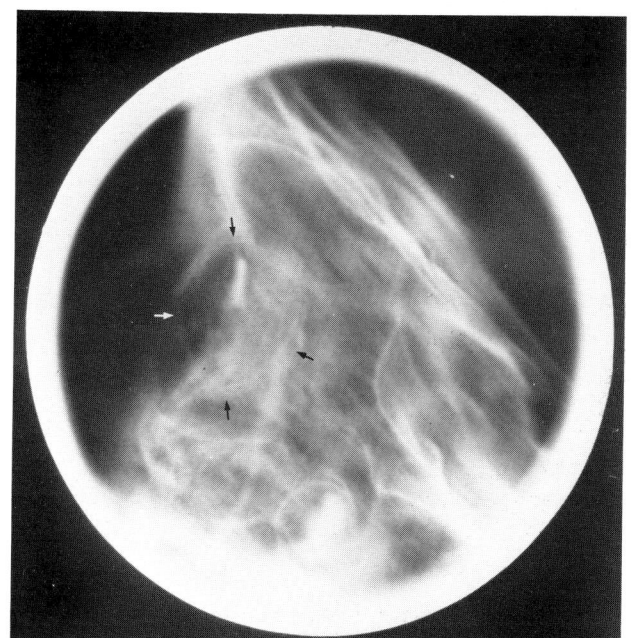

2.5

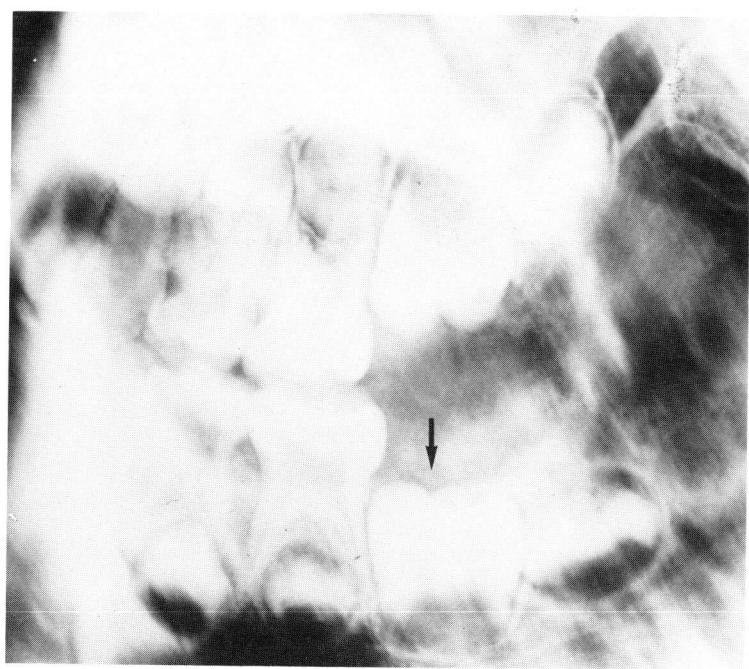

6

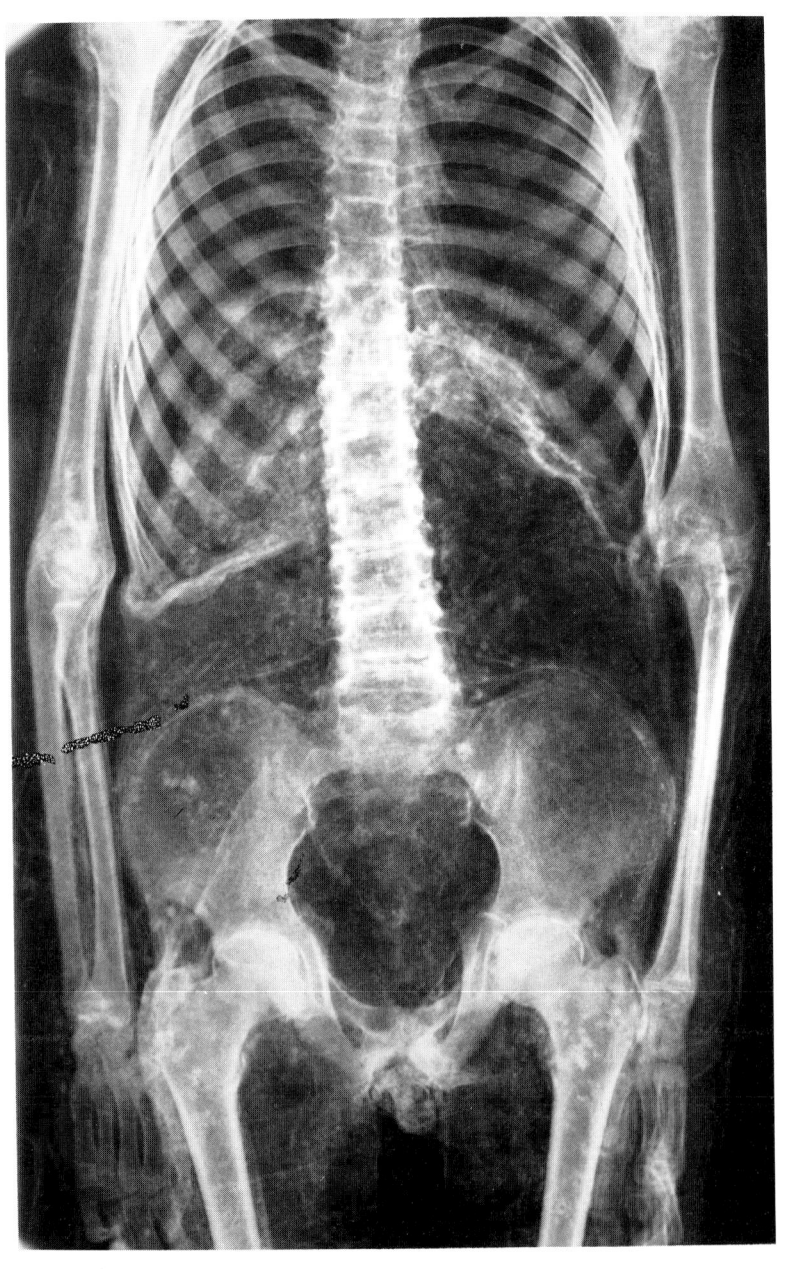

Fig 2.7 Stonyhurst mummy – frontal view of the body shows the
good state of preservation

Harris lines of arrested growth imply babyhood illness but there is no indication of the cause of death.

Salford I

General observations An excellently preserved mummy, 155 cms length, showing no signs of disturbance in the past. The body lies supine with arms extended and hands pronated to rest upon the synphysis pubis. The special feature in this mummy is a curious amulet, which lies in the wrappings over the lower anterior abdominal wall, between the hands and wrists.

Skull All the cranial bones are intact but there is evidence of attempted brain removal via the nose and the cribiform plate. No distinct dural remains are seen but there are several sizeable and mobile rounded opacities clearly visible within the cranial cavity, which may represent brain, resin or a combination of both. The dorsum sellae has been displaced and this delicate flake of bone can be seen, lodged amongst the rounded opacities in the cranium. The eye sockets contain packing and there is a strong possibility that the globe is present on the right side. The nasal cavity is empty but there is packing in the hypopharynx.

Dental state All the teeth are present except the lower right first molar where the root is still in the socket. This tooth would appear to have been missing for a long time, as there is obvious surrounding bone resorption. There is widespread mild attrition in the remaining teeth.

Limbs Arms and legs are complete and articulated with normal joint spaces and with the epiphyses fused. Tomography of the hands shows no signs of any arthritic change. The feet are incomplete – the right first, second and third metatarsals and all the phalanges of both feet are missing.

Thorax The bony thorax is intact and undisturbed, with no rib fractures. The medial end of the clavicle shows an epiphysis which is almost completely fused, indicating an age of under twenty-five years at death. Some of the pleuro-pericardial tissues remain and there is an ovoid opacity in the right paravertebral gutter, at the level of the tenth to twelfth thoracic vertebrae, which would be consistent with residual lung tissue. There is a suggestion of further lung tissue present in the left half of the thoracic cavity.

Abdomen and pelvis No incision site for *post mortem* viscera removal can be detected but there is widespread packaging throughout the

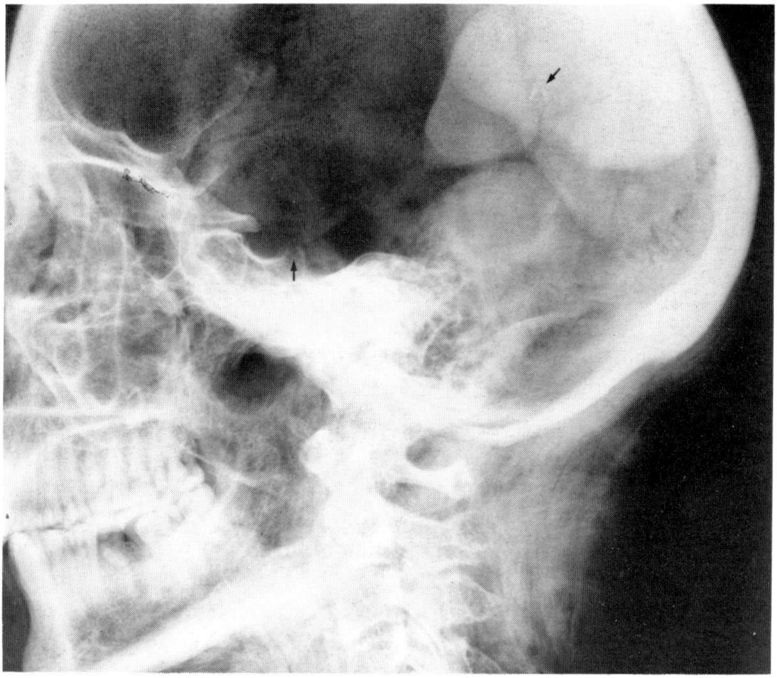

2.8

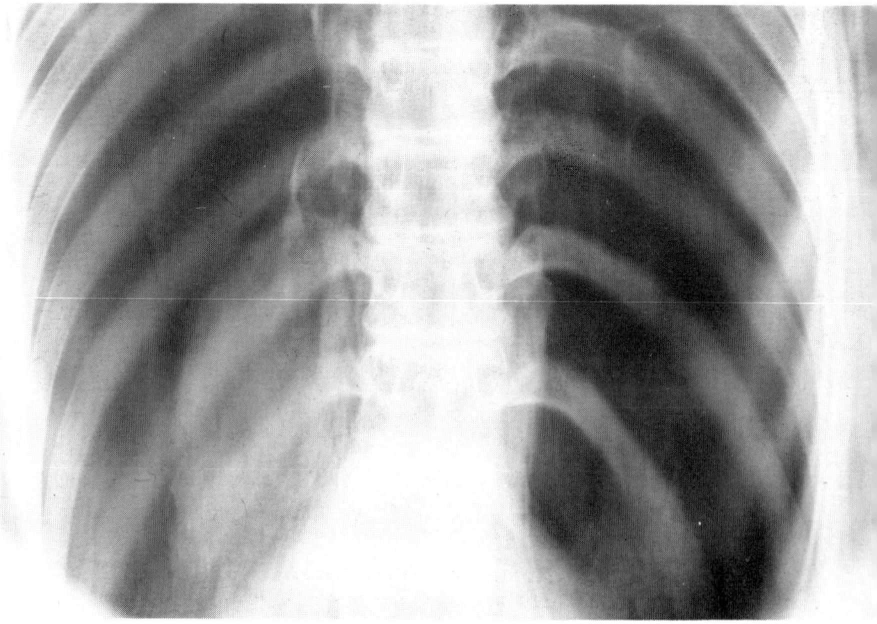

2.9

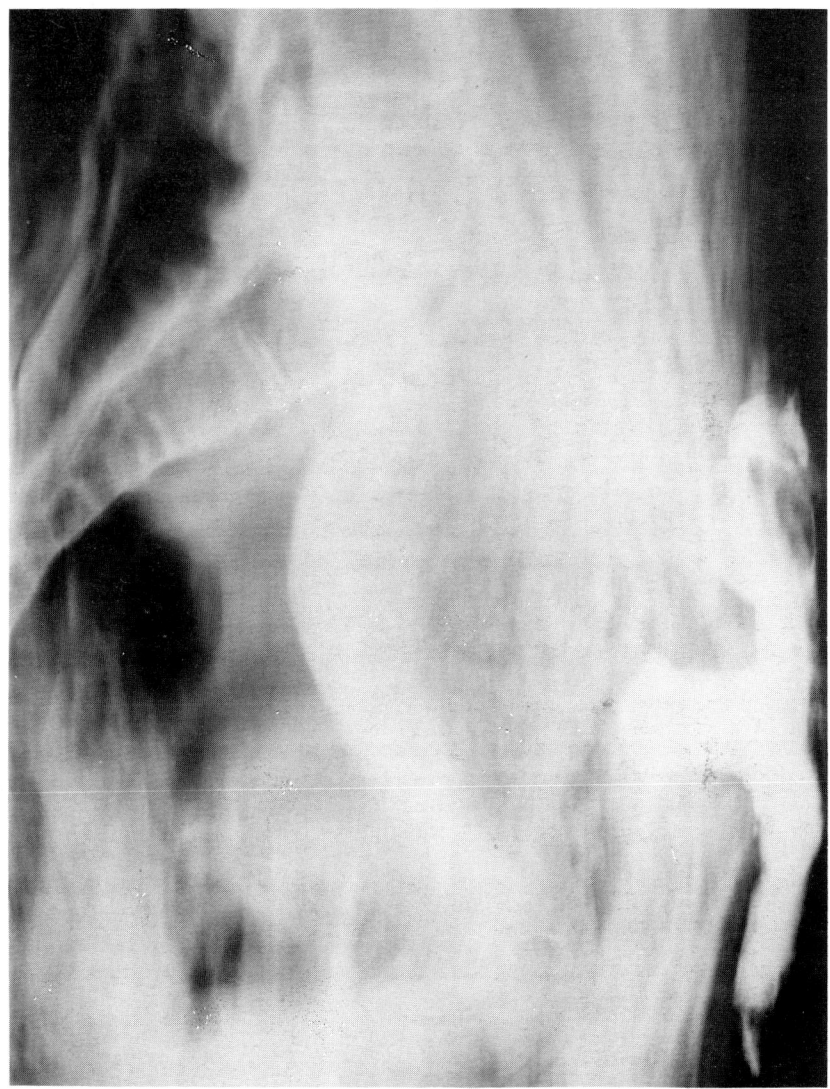

Fig 2.8 Salford I – the large rounded masses in the cranium appear mobile in separate frontal films. The dorsum sellae lies amongst these masses

Fig 2.9 Salford I – frontal tomography of the chest shows lung tissue in the right side of the thorax

Fig 2.10 Salford I – lateral tomography of the pelvis and lower abdomen. The sacral spine lies on the left and the amulet lies in wrappings over the anterior abdominal wall on the right of the figure

abdomen. There is a large linen pack with a smooth outline lying upon the collapsed anterior abdominal wall in the pelvic region. The pelvis shows a female configuration and the iliac crest epiphyses are completely fused. This latter feature implies an age of over twenty years at death.

Spine   This is complete and the well-preserved intervertebral joint spaces show no arthritic changes. The intervertebral discs show some faint opacification.

Comment   This would appear to be the mummy of a young woman of between twenty and twenty-five years of age. The amulet seen in the pelvic region and lying between the wrists is partly metallic and has been the source of much speculation. Computerised tomography has been carried out, but even this technique has failed to establish exactly what it is.

Salford II

General observation   The body of this mummy, which lies supine with arms crossed over the chest, is in a moderate state of preservation. The wrappings show cracks at both knee and ankle level. The head is separated from the trunk at the level of the fifth cervical vertebral. The carpal and metacarpal bones of the right hand lie behind the neck on the left side whilst the fingers lie behind the left humerus. The left scapula is missing as are the anterior ends of some of the left upper ribs. The left clavicle is lying across the middle of the thorax and the left humerus is abnormally rotated, with the left elbow disarticulated.

Skull   The calvarium is intact but there is clear evidence of *post mortem* brain removal through the nose. Part of the nasal septum is absent and there is a defect in the anterior floor of the pituitary fossa. The dorsum sellae is detached and lies behind the clivus, while the posterior clinoid process can be seen in the mid-cranium. There are no dural remains but the presence of multiple resin fluid levels in the posterior part of the cranial cavity is one of the most remarkable features of this mummy. There are faint opaque contents in both eye

Fig 2.11 Salford II skull – a thick later of resin lies posteriorly with a separate rim suggesting movement of the skull while the resin was semi-fluid. Note also the outline of the lower lip

Fig 2.12 Salford II skull – view of the skull base shows resin layering in the cervical spinal canal

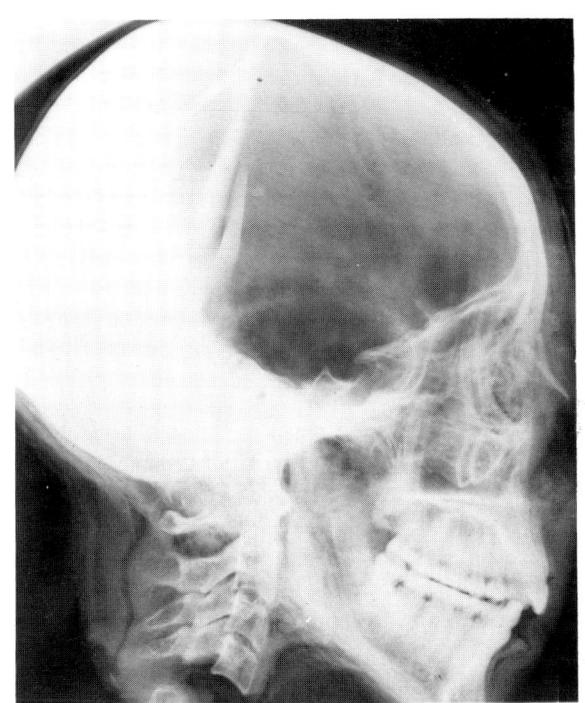

2.11

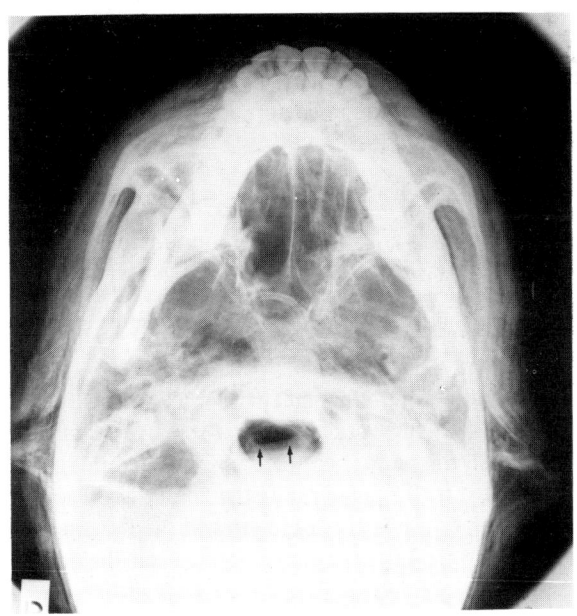

2.12

sockets. A facial profile can just be distinguished at the lower lip level where air is trapped between the face and the wrappings.

Dental state   All permanent teeth are present and in a good state although there is some attrition of all first pre-molars.

Limbs   The upper limbs and the feet are disorganised but despite this all the epiphyses are seen to be fused. The left lateral maleolus is fractured and missing. Linen packing is present between the thighs.

Thorax   The left anterior ribs are fractured and some fragments of these ribs are lying within the chest cavity. There is no evidence of pericardium or lungs remaining within the thorax.

Abodmen and pelvis   A long package lies in the right flank with a further package lying to the left of the left sacroiliac joint, immediately above the pelvic brim. The pelvis itself is female in shape but appears empty.

Spine   The spine is disarticulated at mid-cervical level but is otherwise intact. The x-ray view of the skull base with the attached upper cervical spine shows a fluid level within the spinal canal, similar to those within the cranial cavity. This would indicate the flow of resin into the spinal canal during the process of mummification. There is no opacification of the intervertebral disc material.

Comment   This is a mummy of a young woman. The disorganisation of the bony skeleton would suggest plundering. The most remarkable feature in this mummy is the evidence of brain removal and resin layering in the posterior cranial cavity and in the upper cervical spinal canal.

Salford III

General observations   The body of this mummy lies supine with arms extended. The right arm rests by the lateral aspect of the right thigh and the left arm is pronated and rests on the anterior aspect of the left thigh. The body is in a poor state of preservation – the head is detached, the spine in disarray and the pelvis collapsed.

Skull   The cranial vault is intact with no evidence of brain tissue removal. There is no suggestion of dural remains or of resin.

Dental state   All the permanent teeth are present and erupted except for the wisdom teeth. There is no evidence of significant attrition.

Limbs   The upper limbs are complete and the fingers of both hands are flexed. The lower limbs are also complete but the epiphysis of the left femoral head is displaced. Harris lines of arrested growth are seen

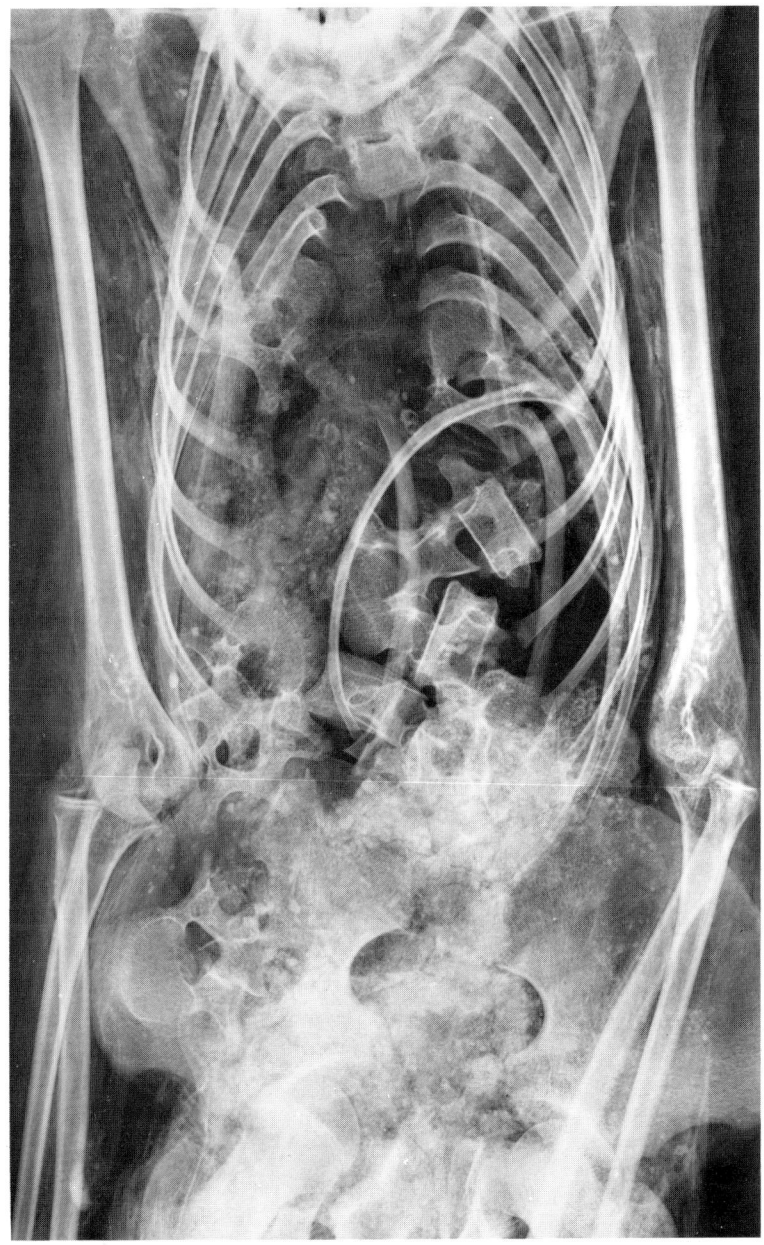

Fig 2.13 Salford III – a poorly preserved mummy with a disorganised
spine and rib cage and collapse of the pelvic girdle

in the distal tibia. There is faint opacification of the menisci in both knee joints. The state of the epiphyses would indicate an age of about fifteen years at the time of death.

Thorax   The mid and lower thoracic spine and ribs are disorganised and there are no contents evident within the thorax.

Abdomen and pelvis   No packaging is seen and the bony pelvis has collapsed in on itself.

Spine   The cervical spine is missing and the thoracic and lumbar spines are disorganised and in disarray.

Comments   The mummified body in a poor state of preservation, is that of a young person of around fifteen years of age at death.

Summary

Protocol for investigation   The current observations are a continuation of the study commenced in 1974, during which the complete collection of Egyptian mummified remains at the Manchester Museum had been radiographed and the findings recorded. During this series of investigations, a protocol was devised which allowed us to reproduce radiographic techniques and to record radiological data. Experience with the initial study has greatly helped the subsequent work. With the inception of the Egyptian Collection Data Bank as a computerised method of recording and cataloging such information, it is essential that such data is collected in a suitable format, and integration and collation of such data would be made very much easier if other investigators involved in such work, adopted the same procedures.

[[3]]

THE ENDOSCOPE IN MUMMY RESEARCH

Endoscopy is a medical technique whereby a narrow tube is introduced through one of the natural orifices of the body or through a small incision in the chest or abdominal wall. The object, of course, is to allow the doctor to see structures which cannot normally be examined and to allow parts of these structures to be removed for subsequent examination under the microscope.

Probably the commonest internal organ to be examined in this way is the stomach in cases where a patient is suspected of having an ulcer. Visualising such ulcers with the endoscope often enables the physician to say whether or not the ulcer is a malignant one (see Fig. 3.2). Moreover, if part of the edge of the ulcer is also removed for histological examination a firm diagnosis can be made in most cases. If the ulcer is not malignant it can be treated medically and therefore the use of endoscopy may spare the patient a major operation. Similar examinations of the rectum and colon are made via the anus whilst it is an everyday occurrence for surgeons to pass endoscopes through the urethra and into the bladder during the investigation of symptoms arising in the urinary tract.

The techniques of medical endoscopy are also used extensively in industry where they enable otherwise inaccesible areas such as those in castings, internal combustion engines and aeroplane wings to be examined for faults. Industrial endoscopes are often known by other names such as borescopes, introscopes and endprobes. As in medicine, they may well save a good deal of time and expense by allowing examinations to be carried out without having to dismatle an engine or other such complicated machinery.

The techniques of endoscopy are very ancient and, indeed, go back to Greek and possibly even ancient Egyptian times. Evidence for the

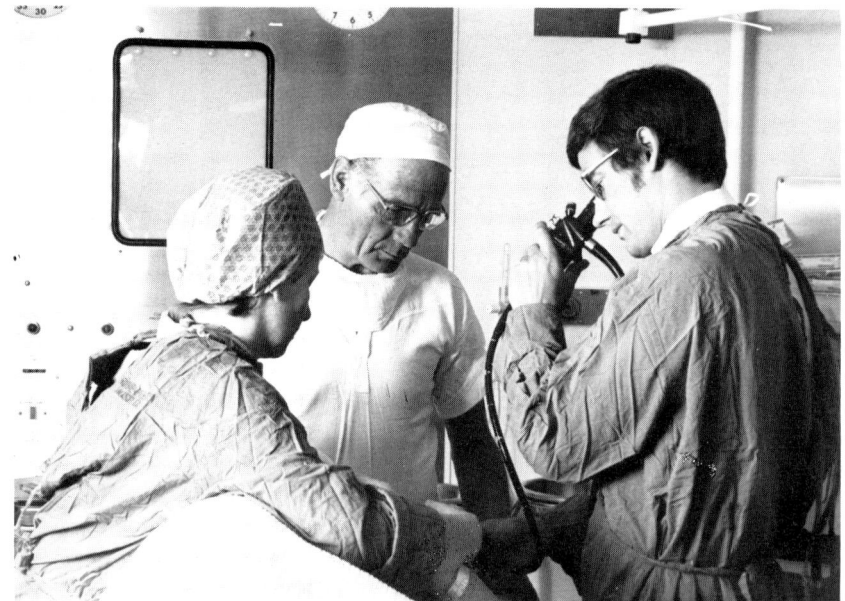

3.1

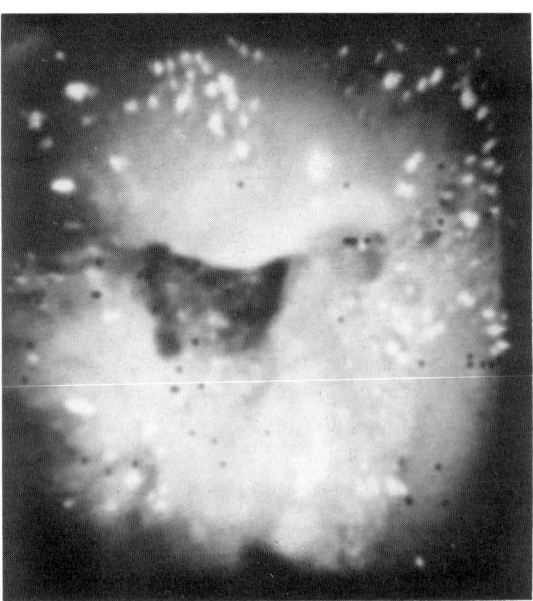

3.2

Fig 3.1 A flexible endoscope is being used to examine the mucosa
lining the stomach

Fig 3.2 A typical benign peptic ulcer visualised with an endoscope.

latter theory comes from an enamelled earthenware statuette dating from the twelfth dynasty which until recently was in the Mariemont Museum.[1] The statuette is of a woman kneeling with her head down between her knees and a man sat down behind her with his hands on her buttocks apparently looking at her anus. This, as might be anticipated, was originally labelled by Egyptologists as an erotic scene, but more recently it has been suggested that it represents a physician performing anoscopy. Certainly it is known that some Egyptian physicians were highly specialised and there may have been some concerned solely with treating diseases of the anus. However the question of whether the title 'Shepherd of the anus' referred to such a specialist or perhaps was someone merely responsible for the royal enemas does not appear to have been resolved so far.

The earliest endoscopes were simple tubes illuminated by either candlelight or sunlight reflected down the tube by a mirror, in much the same way that guides illuminate the ancient Egyptian tombs for the modern visitor.

In the later part of the last century a further development was the use of a lamp, not dissimilar to a miner's hat lamp, worn on the head of the surgeon so that the beam of light would be directed down the tube. A further development was the use of a slotted mirror which reflected the light down the tube in parallel rays whilst the user looked through the gaps in the mirror.

Later, a small electric light bulb was incorporated into the probing end of the endoscope although, as might be expected, the heat from the bulb added to the discomfort from which the patient was already suffering due to the endoscope itself. One must bear in mind of course that these early instruments measured up to one inch in diameter. Subsequent developments in the early part of this century included the incorporation of small diameter lenses into the tube with mirrors or prisms at the probing end to enable the user to look sideways at areas not able to be seen through the direct viewing instruments. It was not however until the 1950s that a principle first demonstrated by John Tyndall in 1870 at the Royal Society in London was incorporated into the endoscope. This basic principle was that a stream of water flowing from an illuminated vessel conducted light by the phenomena of total internal reflection. This principle when applied to a strand of glass coated with glass of a different refractive index resulted in the term fibre optics. When a bundle of these strands bonded in resin was incorporated into an endoscope light could be transmitted along them from a remote source, consequently its voltage could be increased and far better vision could be obtained without any discomfort to the patient caused by excess heat. The next stage in the development was to manufacture a bundle of the fibres in such a way that each fibre was in the same geometric position at each end. The ends of the fibres were polished and lens systems incorporated to focus an image on one end and a viewing eyepiece on the other. This part could then be used to examine the desired area whilst a random bundle of fibres was also included to illuminate the area to be viewed. This instrument was, for obvious reasons, called a fibrescope. Its flexibility proved quite remarkable in that it would still transmit images even when bent around corners, thus opening up new horizons in viewing the internal organs of the body. The early instruments suffered with broken fibres in the bundles, resulting in black dots in the image and also from slight lack of flexibility; nevertheless, they represented a great breakthrough in the field of endoscopy.

During the past fifteen years great advances have been made. The probing tip of a medical fibrescope may now be manipulated by controls at the proximal end so that it points in any direction, giving the physician much more control over his examination. Additional chan-

Fig 3.3 The controls at the proximal end of the endoscope allow the tip to be pointed in the desired direction

nels have been introduced so that blood or fluid which is obscuring the part to be examined may be sucked out and biopsy forceps have been incorporated to enable tissue to be taken for examination under the microscope. The present medical fibrescopes have a working length of up to 2.5 m and diameters as small as 2.4 mm. Rigid medical endo-scopes have, of course, a smaller working length (up to 50 cm) but may be obtained with similar small diameters, whilst industrial instruments have diameters which go down to 1.7 mm.

It is, of course, this modern range of instruments which have proved so useful in the investigations of the Manchester mummies. Whilst in recent years a good deal of knowledge about mummification and disease in ancient Egypt has been gained from the examination of Egyptian mummies by normal autopsy techniques, these methods inevitably result in destruction of material which can never be replaced. With this in mind, during the past four years, attempts have been made in Manchester to develop non-destructive techniques of examination, which would provide material for histopathological examination and yet leave priceless specimens unspoiled for museum display purposes and undamaged for posterity.

In the first instance attempts were made to take specimens from the inside of mummies by the use of narrow hollow needles of the type used in medicine for liver and renal biopsy work. These were not satisfactory as they depend to a certain extent on the slight movement of the organ to be sampled into a groove in the needle. Clearly, dry and very rigid liver or renal tissue in Egyptian mummies was not amenable to removal in this way.

Later, a larger hollow needle – in fact a tube with a diameter of some 0.5 cm was obtained. This had a cutting edge at one end and attempts were made with this instrument to obtain solid cores of mummy tissue. Whilst a certain amount of tissue was obtained using this technique, the dry crumbling nature of mummified tissue did not lend itself in many instances to the acquisition of satisfactory samples and it was at this point that it was decided to explore the technique of endoscopy.

By a pure coincidence at about the same time that one of the editors was attempting to persuade his gastroenterological colleagues at Preston Infirmary to lend him one of their endoscopes to use on the mummies, the other gave a lecture to the Institute of Chartered Surveyors where someone suggested the use of an industrial borescope of the type used by surveyors to examine the inside of cavity walls. Keymed (Medical

Industrial Instruments) Ltd, of Southend, make, as their name suggests, endoscopes for use in both the medical and industrial fields and
readily agreed to co-operate with the editors to investigate their use in
Egyptian mummies. Since that time, their local salesman, Ken Wildsmith, has become an enthusiastic member of the team in Manchester
giving much of his spare time to help with the project and in particular
has been responsible for all the photographs taken through the
instruments.

For endoscopy to succeed in Egyptian mummies it will be clear that
the tissue to be visualised inside the body must have an air filled space
on at least one aspect, into which the endoscope can be introduced.
They cannot, therefore, be used, as they are in medicine, to examine
the gastrointestinal tract or bladder where the pathways have collapsed
and cannot, as in the living patient, be expanded by the introduction of
air. They have, however, been introduced into mummies by less
conventional routes and have indeed proved to be extremely useful in
several areas where they have yielded valuable information concerning
both mummification and disease in ancient Egypt.

As the lungs were often removed by the Egyptian embalmers and the
thoracic cavity left empty, the latter seemed a worthwhile site at which
to begin to explore the use of endoscopic techniques. It was with this in
mind that our attention turned to the mummy of Asru, which has been
the subject of previous investigations by the team. When the bandages
were removed from Asru some years ago her intestines were found lying
between her legs and examination of these revealed that she suffered
from a parasitic worm infestation of the Strongyloides species.[2] There
was no evidence of an incision in the abdominal wall and the embalmers
appeared to have removed the intestine and other internal organs
through the pelvic floor. The anatomy of the anus and vagina could not
be established with certainty but in the dried state there appeared to be
a common orifice through which the organs had been extracted. X-Rays
of the chest showed radio-opaque tissue which, it was thought,
probably represented collapsed lung or the heart in the central part of
the chest, but the thoracic cavities appeared to be empty. The skin and
subcutaneous tissue on the chest wall were of a hard leathery consistency but two holes each less than 1 cm in diameter were bored through the
chest wall from the back on either side and a variety of rigid industrial
endoscopes were used to examine the thoracic cavity (see Fig. 3.4). An
excellent view of the inside of the thorax was obtained and, as suspected

from the X-Rays, the lungs were collapsed down to the midline. There was no evidence of resin within the chest. The thin membrane (pleura) lining the inside of the cavity and the underlying ribs could be seen quite clearly, and appeared to be free from disease. The back bone could be visualised and showed no evidence of disease. Part of the diaphragm, the thin layer of muscle separating the chest and abdominal cavities could be seen and appeared to have been damaged at one point, presumably when the embalmers removed the contents of the abdomen.

Radiographs of the collapsed lung tissue showed peculiar striped markings and it was of considerable interest to find out what these were, in addition to looking for evidence of disease in the lung. Consequently small retrieval forceps attached to the endoscope and manipulated from outside the chest were used to take samples from the suspected lung tissue. Direct visualisation of the tip of the endoscope on a radiographic screen was used to position the endoscope within the chest so that the biopsy could be taken more exactly from the desired site (see Fig. 3.5). The histological examination of this tissue is described in detail elsewhere but at this point it is worthwhile pointing out that it showed scarring of the pleura and the lung tissue as well as revealing that not only did Asru suffer from a *Strongyloides* infestation but that a quite different parasitic worm, *Ecchinococcus*, had given rise to a Hydatid cyst within the lung. The examination of Asru was continued by introducing the endoscope through the common anal/ vaginal orifice. Unfortunately the view was limited by the absence of air within the abdomen. The latter had been emptied by the embalmers and consequently the anterior abdominal wall had collapsed backwards and obliterated the cavity. Biopsies were taken of muscle and blood vessels from the wall of the pelvic cavity although histological examination of these specimens did not reveal any significant abnormalities.

Finally, attempts were made to examine the inside of Asru's skull. In some mummies it has been possible to pass endoscopes up the nose and through the defect in the base of the skull made by the embalmers. Unfortunately this was not possible with Asru, as the soft tissue in her nose had collapsed and blocked this route. However, the eye sockets were empty and the hole in the back of the socket through which the optic nerve enters the brain was patent, so it was possible to pass a narrow-bore rigid industrial instrument through this hole and obtain a satisfactory view of the inside of the skull. There appeared to be some

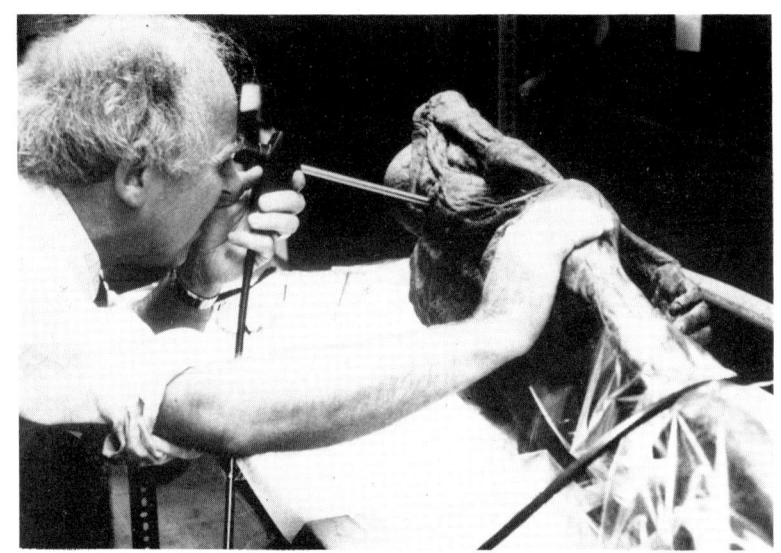

3.4

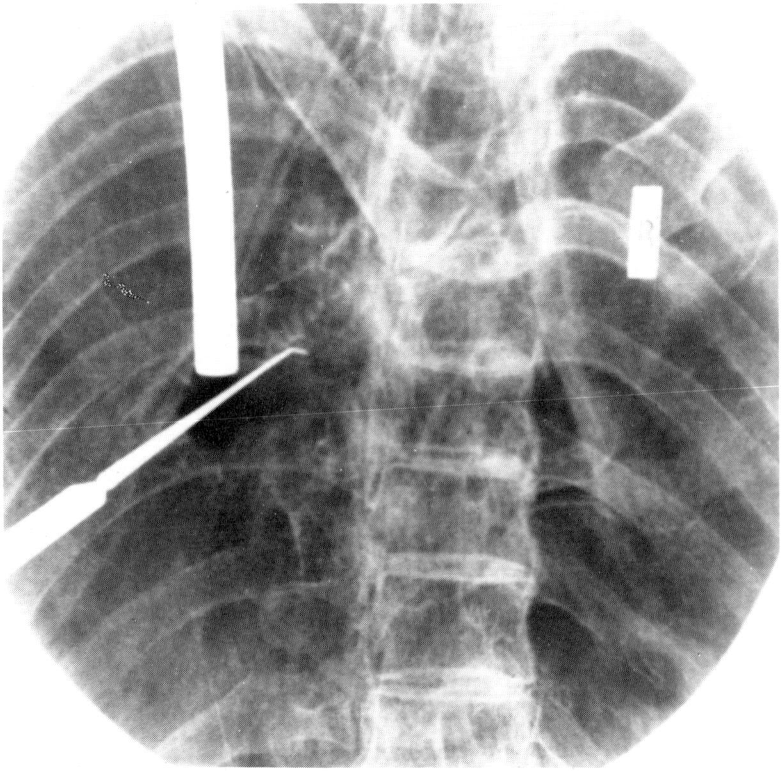

3.5

brain tissue in the back of the skull but it was not possible to biopsy this due to the small size of the access hole. A burr hole similar to that described in mummy skull 22940 will be necessary if Asru's brain is to be examined histologically. Several intact larval skins were seen lying free within the skull and these, after being photographed through the endoscope, were removed with fine retrieval forceps. They appeared to be very similar to those examined previously from Asru's intestines and identified as *Chrysomyia*.[3]

Khary was the second mummy to be investigated by endoscopic techniques. This mummy was still bandaged and therefore, as the normal external landmarks of the body were obscured, it presented an even more severe test of the endoscopic techniques. However small holes, were made in the chest wall with minimal damage to the bandages and endoscopes of various types were again used to obtain a view of the inside of the chest. The appearances, however, were quite different from those in Asru. The lungs were only partially collapsed and in some places they were attached to the pleura over the rib cage (see Fig. 3.6). These adhesions are usually the result of inflammation in the lungs and pleura during life. When they are present, they prevent the lungs from collapsing completely as the air is gradually absorbed from them after death. They prevented one from seeing across from one side of the chest cavity to the other and in fact divided the chest cavity into three sections. There was a good deal of resin on the surface of the lungs but using the endoscope and biopsy forceps it was possible to examine several areas and to take biopsies for histological examination. Microscopy of this tissue proved to be interesting and, as will be described in detail later, showed evidence of sand pneumoconiosis similar to that seen in the mummy Nekht Ankh.

The collection of Egyptian mummy material in Manchester includes several isolated heads, many of which have now been investigated using endoscopic techniques, and interesting information has been obtained concerning both embalming procedures and disease. This part of the investigation has been assisted greatly by the help and advice of Peter Stanworth, a consultant neurosurgeon. Radiological studies have

Fig 3.4 A rigid endoscope is being used to examine the inside of Asru's chest

Fig 3.5 The tip of the endoscope can be seen close to the part of the lung showing striped markings and from which a biopsy is required

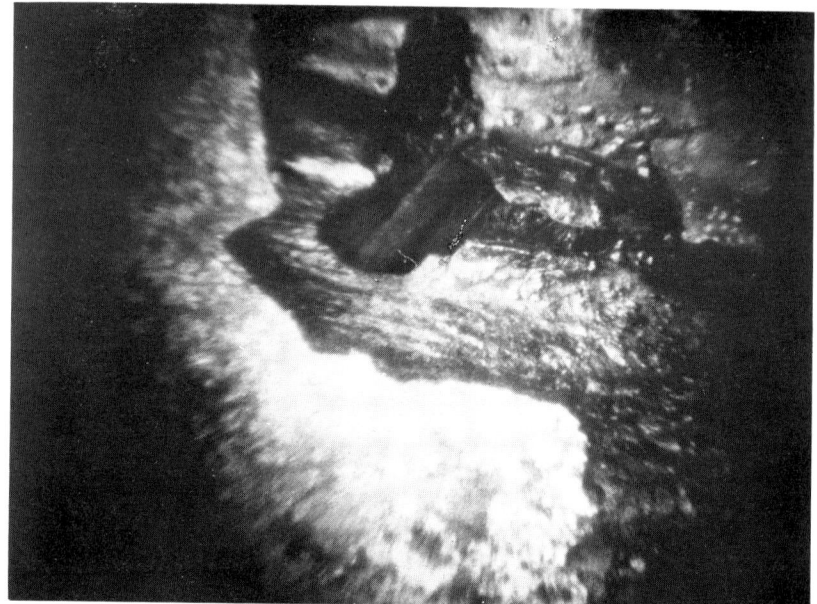

3.6

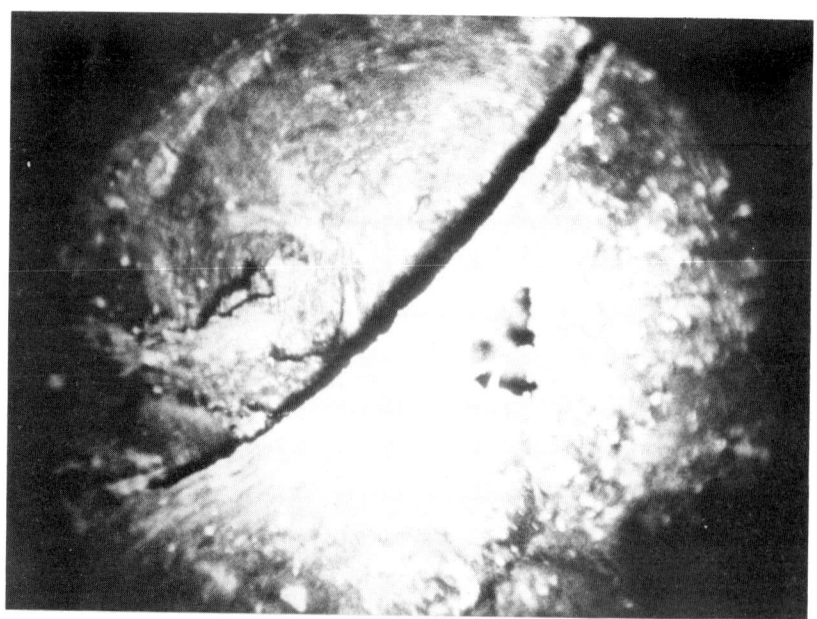

3.7

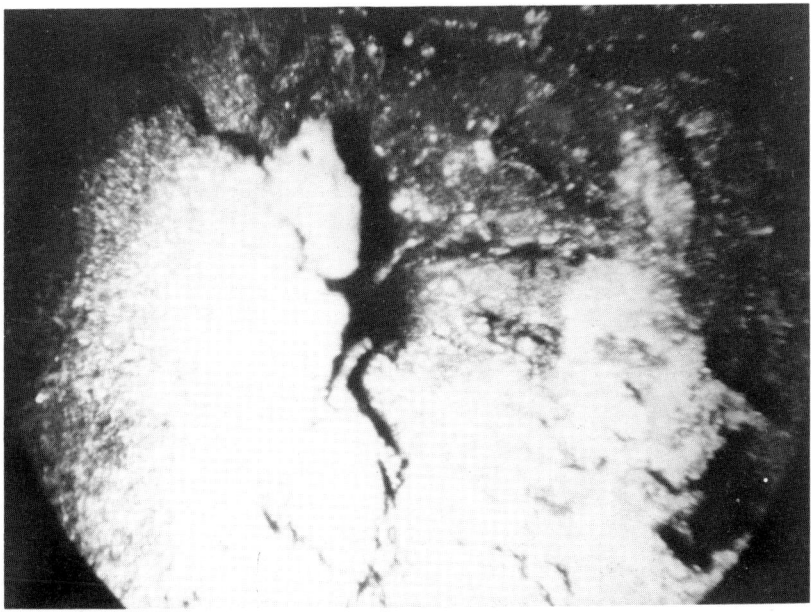

Fig 3.6 Collapsed lung tissue within Khary's chest is visualised with the endoscope

Fig 3.7 The edge of the bone separating the anterior and middle cranial fossae can be seen through an endoscope introduced into the skull via the nose

Fig 3.8 The surface of the radiological fluid level is seen through the endoscope to be irregular and fissured

shown previously that in many mummies there are defects in the base of the skull, which presumably have been made by the embalmers when they introduced instruments up the nose and into the skull in order to remove the brain.[4] It was common practice for this process to be left for a few days after death so that *post mortem* autolysis would cause some liquifaction of the brain, making it easier to extract by this route. In some instances resin was introduced into the skull by the same route in order to aid preservation of the body. It was hoped that by examining the skulls endoscopically we might learn more about these procedures.

In some instances, the defect in the base of the skull provided a pathway for the endoscope. As this route was sometimes tortuous, flexible endoscopes were of particular value. As the endoscope was introduced through the nose there was often a good view of the pathway ahead and the defect in the base of the skull could be visualised. As the endoscope emerged through this into the cavity of the skull a general view of the anterior part of the cavity (anterior cranial fossa) could be seen and as the instrument was moved around, the membranes lining the skull and dividing it into compartments (falx cerebri and tentorium cerebelli) could also be visualised. In addition, the central part of the cavity (middle cranial fossa) could be seen (Fig. 3.7). It was often possible to see the groove on these bones in which during life the middle meningeal artery was situated. This vessel is important in that it often gets damaged when the side of the skull is fractured, and this may lead to a very dangerous haemorrhage which quickly threatens life if it is not stopped by the neurosurgeon.

The instrument could then be manipulated so that it points backwards towards the posterior cranial fossa and the area of the base of the skull which encloses the pituitary gland (sella tursica) could be seen. The bone behind the pituitary gland (dorsum sellae) protrudes from the base of the skull and consequently was in danger of being damaged by the ancient Egyptian embalmers, when they introduced their instruments. Radiologically, in the Ptolemaic mummy head (5275) it was suspected that this might have occurred and the bone have been displaced. Using the endoscope it was possible to see the displaced bone, in this case embedded in either resin or brain tissue at the back of the skull where it had been pushed by the embalmers some two thousand years before.

It has been mentioned previously that this mode of entry into the skull is not always available, and the eye socket provided the answer with Asru. In isolated mummy heads it was sometimes possible to introduce flexible endoscopes through the space within the bones of the neck which normally contains the spinal cord (vertebral canal). Passing an endoscope upwards through this passage has allowed access to the cranial cavity through the so-called foramen magnum where in life the brain merges with the spinal cord. This method proved valuable, as will be seen later in the case of mummy head 1981/575.

It should be pointed out that the endoscope has been of particular value in investigating the so called 'fluid' levels seen radiologically in several skulls. Through the endoscope one can see that in some instances these 'fluid' levels have a smooth flat surface and indeed when the material forming these is biopsied it is found to consist of resin. The position of these resin levels indicate that the body lay prone for some time after the resin was poured in, and indeed there was time for it to set hard before the body was moved. In the case of mummy head 1981/575 the resin level showed that the body was propped up at an angle from the horizontal during the mummification procedure. Further information concerning radiological fluid levels was also obtained from the endoscopic examination, for in some instances the surface of the fluid level was irregular and fissured (see Fig. 3.8). In these cases, biopsies showed that the substance forming the fluid level was indeed decomposing brain. It was clear in these instances that the brain had been incompletely removed and, as it liquified it had sunk to the back of the skull, forming the fluid level. The body must have been left prone for a considerable time as the brain must have dried out and rehardened in this position for the 'fluid' level to have persisted after the body had been moved.

Finally, in one head where none of the routes into the skull mentioned so far was available, a burr hole was made by Peter Stanworth using the kind of tools which he uses every day to carry out neurosurgical operations. These tools consist of a brace and bit very similar to that used by carpenters. The drill hole normally made by the neurosurgeon is about 1 cm in diameter and during an operation he may make several of these around an area of the skull which he wishes to remove in order to operate on the brain beneath. In mummy head 22940, one burr hole made through an area of the skull, shown radiologically to be away from brain tissue, was sufficient. An endoscope introduced through it enabled one to obtain an excellent view of the interior of the skull and in this particular case was most valuable as it allowed a brain biopsy to be taken. As will be seen later, the histological examination of this biopsy showed evidence of a Hydatid cyst and it is clear that this ancient Egyptian suffered, like Asru, from an *Ecchinococcus* worm infestation.

[4]

DISEASE AND THE MANCHESTER MUMMIES: THE PATHOLOGIST'S ROLE

Pathology is the branch of medicine which deals with the scientific study of disease processes. It is concerned first of all with aetiology, that is, with the factors which cause or initiate disease and those which cause it to progress or get worse. Of course, the factors which cause disease are many and unfortunately in some instances, as with the major killer disease, cancer, the factors are still incompletely understood. On the other hand, the infectious diseases, which have been with us from the earliest times and were certainly known to occur in ancient Egypt, are known to be due to micro-organisms which attack the body. The study of these organisms now involves several subspecialities within pathology and it is largely due to the efforts of microbiologists, virologists, bacteriologists and parasitologists that many of the organisms causing these diseases have been isolated and identified. The latter is clearly an important stage in the scientific study of such diseases and one which is often essential before a specific treatment can be found.

The part played by microbiologists in the investigation of ancient Egyptian remains has been limited so far to the identification of organisms found in the mummified tissue when it is examined under the microscope. Attempts have been made to isolate live organisms using the elaborate techniques of the speciality but so far these have been of no avail. However, further attempts should, perhaps continue to be made since it is known that some organisms may exist in a dormant stage as spores for many years and such spores have certainly been seen down the microscope.[1]

Pathology is also concerned with the diagnosis and monitoring of disease processes. In addition to microbiology, a number of subspecialities have developed within pathology to study these factors. The branch of haematology is concerned with diseases associated with the formed elements of blood. These erythrocytes (red cells), leucocytes (white cells) and platelets play an important part in many normal and disease processes within the body. They may change in number and appearance in primary blood diseases such as leukaemia or anaemia and also in response to other disease processes such as infections within the body. It is obvious, however, that the scope for haematology in the study of Egyptian mummies is somewhat limited by the lack of fluid blood. On the other hand, some progress has been made in the past few years in recognising individual blood elements within tissue sections, at both light and electron optical levels. In earlier studies there was some confusion between fungal spores and red cells but elegant scanning electron microscope studies of both red and white cells from mummified tissue have now been published.[2]

Closely allied to haematology is the study of blood group serology. This discipline is concerned with the specific substances found in the red cells and in the serum of blood which enables a specific blood group to be assigned to a particular individual. This work will be described in more detail elsewhere in this book.

Chemical pathology is concerned with the analysis and quantitation of the various substances within blood, urine and other body fluids. Normal constituents of these fluids may vary in health and disease and chemical pathology consequently gives vital information to the physician concerning both the diagnosis and monitoring of disease. However, like haematology, the scope of chemical pathology is limited in Egyptian mummies by the absence of body fluid. On the other hand attempts have been made to analyse the chemical constituents of mummified tissue, although here the analyses may be confused by natron used in mummification diffusing into the tissue. However, some large molecular weight substances such as lipoproteins and proteolipids have been isolated and studied.[3] Abnormal chemicals, including poisons, may also be detected in the tissues of the body and perhaps these give the greatest scope for investigation in ancient Egyptian material. Except for analyses of the lead and mercury content of bone, little work has been done in this direction.[3] There is no doubt however, that the detection in mummified tissue of poisons, such as arsenic and heavy metals, such as lead, is worthy of further study.

As might be anticipated, the branches of pathology which have given most information concerning disease in Egyptian mummies are those of morbid anatomy and histopathology. The knowledge gained through these disciplines has been expanded during the past twenty years by the use of the electron microscope and more recently by new immunohistochemical techniques.

Morbid anatomy involves the naked eye study of whole mummies by conventional autopsy methods supplemented by the study of parts of mummies which may become available from time to time. This began with the 'unrolling' and examination of mummies during the last century but reached a more scientific level with the detailed examination of the Two Brothers by Margaret Murray and her team in Manchester at the beginning of the century.[4] Excavation in Egypt at this time was in its heyday and during this period many mummies were examined on or close by the excavation site.

By far the largest number of bodies to be examined as a group were the six thousand or so reported by Elliot-Smith and Wood Jones in their archaeological survey of the Nubia.[5] Most of the bodies in this survey consisted merely of bones and there were only a few instances where the cause of death could be ascertained. As might be anticipated, evidence of trauma in the form of fractures of bones was common although they comment on the relative absence of sepsis in them. Indeed, they came to the conclusion that inflammatory diseases of bone were relatively rare in ancient Egypt. There is no doubt from other studies that tuberculosis of bone occurred during this period, the bones examined from Nagada showing undisputed evidence of tuberculosis. Some of the Nagada bones may be pre-dynastic but certainly the latest is thought to date from before 1300 BC.[6] The commonest disease found in ancient Egyptian bones was arthritis.[7] Osteoarthritis, essentially a wear and tear disease of the joint, was by far the most prevalent. Various congenital diseases of bone such as achondroplasia, cleft palate and hydrocephalus have also been discovered in the skeletons from ancient Egypt.[8] The absence of evidence of neoplasia is very obvious in the large surveys of bones and indeed, there are very few recorded cases of either primary or secondary tumours in bone. Possible primary tumours of bone have been recorded, but in general the correct diagnosis in these cases is in doubt since they have not been subjected to histological examination.[9] The absence of secondary tumours in bone which have spread from cancers at other sites in the body is very striking but is probably related to the younger age group of the population being studied.

Morbid anatomical examinations of small groups of mummies or even isolated specimens have also contributed to our knowledge of disease in ancient Egypt, and in some of these, soft tissues have also been available for examination. In such material gall stones and renal stones have been found, as well as a possible case of appendicitis. Other examples include unilateral hypoplasia of the kidney, megacolon and scrotal hernias whilst gynaecological and obstetrical conditions, including vaginal prolapses, have also been noted.[10]

Whilst these morbid anatomical observations have given rise to a good deal of knowledge about disease in ancient Egypt, they are incomplete and there is usually some doubt about diagnosis unless they are combined with histological studies. Whilst occasional workers in the last century had attempted to examine mummified tissue under the microscope,[11] it was Ruffer, in 1911, who was the first to combine morbid anatomical techniques with microscopical examination of the tissues and therefore open up a completely new dimension in the study of disease in Egyptian mummies.[12] One of his most remarkable discoveries was identification of calcified ova of *Bilharzia* in the kidneys of two twentieth dynasty mummies.[13] Interestingly, this parasitic infestation is still a major problem in Egypt today, affecting some forty per cent of the population. Unfortunately, relatively few workers followed Ruffer's lead and between the wars only Simandl[14] who examined skin and striated muscle, and Shaw,[15] who carried out a more extensive histological examination of tissue from the mummy of the singer Har-mose (eighteenth dynasty) are of note. This mummy was extremely well preserved, and the changes in the lung suggested a diagnosis of bronchopneumonia.

Renewed interest in the use of histological techniques was stimulated by Sandison's work between 1955 and his untimely death in 1982.[16] Sandison's modification of Ruffer's techniques were used by Rowling in his MD thesis *Disease in Ancient Egypt*[17], and served as a stimulant to the present workers who use methods which, in some instances, were derived from his.[18]

The past ten years has been a particularly fruitful period for the study of disease in Egyptian mummies, several groups of workers combining morbid anatomical techniques with those of histology, histochemistry and electron microscopy. The detailed examination of Mummy 1770 in Manchester,[19] PUM II in Detroit and ROM I in Toronto[20] have been particularly outstanding.

The most interesting finding, common to all three mummies, was the

presence of parasitic infestations. Mummy 1770 was infected with
guinea worm (*Dracunculus medinensis*). The latter is acquired by
drinking water containing immature forms of the parasites which
develop in the stomach and later burrow through to the abdominal wall
where they mate. The male then dies and indeed, it was the death of the
male a significant period before the death of 1770 which led to it being
preserved naturally by the calcium which had been deposited in it.
Moreover, the calcium in the worm made it radio-opaque and in fact
the calcified nodule in the abdominal wall had been noted on radiography of the mummy prior to autopsy. The pregnant female, which is
much larger than the male, tends to wander through the tissues of the
body and usually settles in the legs, where the irritation it causes results
in ulceration. The worm then lays its eggs through the ulcer and these
get into water where they lie ready to infect another person. The legs of
1770 had been amputated shortly before or at death and therefore
evidence of this part of the worm's life cycle is missing. Although the
amputations did not appear to be surgical, it is interesting to speculate
that they were connected with the worm infestation.

PUM II also showed evidence of a parasitic infestation, in this
instance a round worm called *Ascaris*. This is a very common parasite in
tropical and subtropical countries where a large proportion of the
population is affected. Infection, as with the guinea worm, occurs when
immature forms are ingested. The larvae hatch in the small intestine,
penetrate the wall and eventually reach the lungs. From there they
migrate along the airways and down the gullet, so regaining the
intestine where they mature into adults. Eggs are laid which, if they get
into soil, are again ready to infect the next victim.

ROM I, a weaver by the name of Nakht, proved an even more
fruitful source of parasites, for not only did he have a *bilharzia*
infestation but the intercostal muscle revealed a cyst originating from a
trichinella infestation, whilst the intestine contained eggs of a *Taenia*
species. Both the latter parasites are of particular interest in that they
are associated with eating meat and *Trichinella* in particular with pork.
Infection with *Trichinella* occurs when undercooked pork containing
immature forms is eaten. These develop into adult worms in the
intestine and the female penetrates the wall, where she may deposit up
to 1500 larvae. These may get into every organ of the body but only
become encysted in striated muscle, hence the finding of one in the
muscle between the ribs. *Taenia* is a flat worm which infects man in the

same way as *Trichinella*. Two species are found, and infection may occur from undercooked beef (*Taenia sagginata*) or undercooked pork (*Taenia solium*). The finding of *Trichinella* and *Taenia* in Nakht certainly indicates that the ancient Egyptians were not strict vegetarians and moreover that, at least at some periods of the year, they ate pork. It has been suggested that as the pig is associated with Seth in the Osiris legend it may well be that pork was only eaten at certain times of the year.[21] It is interesting to speculate that the religious prohibition of pork which goes back to ancient Egyptian times may originally have had a hygienic basis, although of course a specific association between pork and *Trichinella* infestation was not recognised until the middle of the last century.

Since these autopsies were carried out, work in Manchester has progressed in several ways. Histological and electron optical findings in previously examined material has been reviewed as newer techniques become available. Additional new material from specimens has been examined and, most importantly, a good deal of new and exciting material has become available for these studies through the endoscopic techniques described elsewhere. In addition to the histological techniques, details of which have been published,[22] new tissue stains of the conventional type as well as new histochemical stains have been used. Conventional histochemical stains depend on the reaction of a chemical in the stain with a chemical in the section, the stain pinpointing the presence of a particular chemical substance in the tissue. The newer histochemical stains used in the present work depend on a specific immunological reaction between a particular protein in the tissue (the antigen) and its specific antibody which is attached to a visible dye in the stain. These immunohistochemical stains may be applied widely for the detection of specific substances within the tissues but at the moment are limited to some extent by the range of antibodies available. However, more antibodies are becoming available all the time and it is hoped that the work done so far in Manchester will encourage investigators at other centres to explore the use of these stains in mummified material.

The electron microscope is being used increasingly in the study of Ancient Egyptian mummies. There are now records in the literature of bone, cartilage, skin, muscle, bacteria and blood cells being examined by transmission electron microscopy.[23] Previous studies in Manchester have demonstrated its usefulness in some of these fields and in addition it was used to examine a well preserved liver found in a canopic jar belonging to Nekht Ankh. This specimen was particularly valuable as the cell membranes and cell membrane junctions (desmosomes) could be identified. The nuclei of cells could also be seen and in one cell part of the mechanism of cell division was demonstrated.

Analytical electron microscopy is a technique whereby the elements in a tissue at a particular spot can be analysed and quantified. The Manchester team were the first to apply this technique in mummy research and were able to show that particles in the lung of the mummy of Nekht Ankh contained a high proportion of silica and were probably sand particles.

Scanning electron microscopy whereby the surface of an object can be examined at an electron optical level is also proving of use and it has been used in America for the study of hair and blood cells. In Manchester, attempts have been made to use it to characterise hair from the mummies of the two half brothers, Nekht Ankh and Khnum Nakht. In addition it was used to help in identifying many of the insects which have been found in and on the mummies from the Manchester Museum.[24]

The application and usefulness of the newer techniques of both light and electron microscopy may perhaps be demonstrated best by considering in more detail four quite different organs of the body which have been studied amongst many others from the Manchester Museum.

The skin is an interesting and vital organ of the body as it protects internal organs from the environment. By the same token, however, it was also in the closest contact with the materials which ancient Egyptians used to aid mummification. The natron which they used would dehydrate the skin and cause shrinkage. However, preservation under these circumstances has been demonstrated to be quite good and providing gentle rehydration is carried out, satisfactory histological sections can be prepared. On the other hand, when resins were used it is believed that they were applied hot in a molten state. In addition to damaging the skin they made the skin stick to the overlying bandages and hence when the latter are removed the skin is often removed also. Being the closest organ to the exterior environment the skin also suffers from organisms entering it and infecting it after death. This may have occured in the early stages before it was wrapped, whilst it was in the tomb or indeed, at a much later stage in a museum if conservation was inadequate. Examples of bacteriological and fungal infestation have

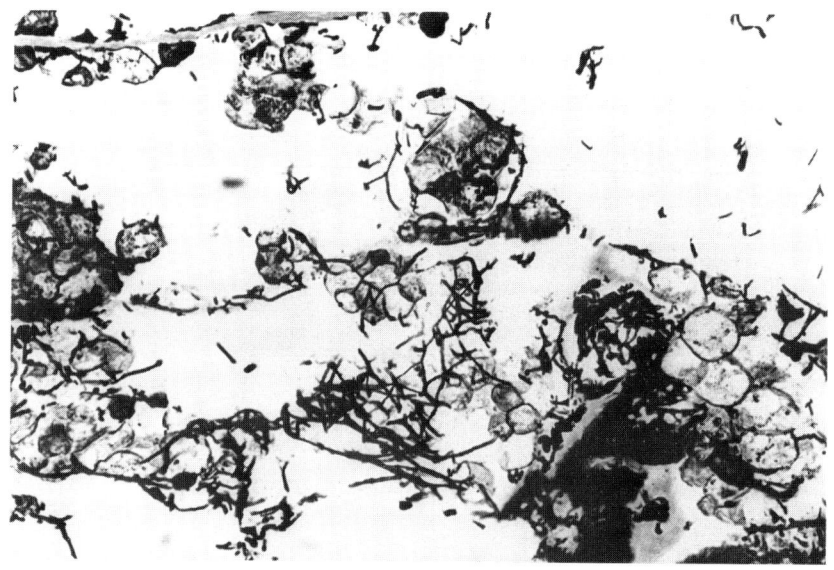

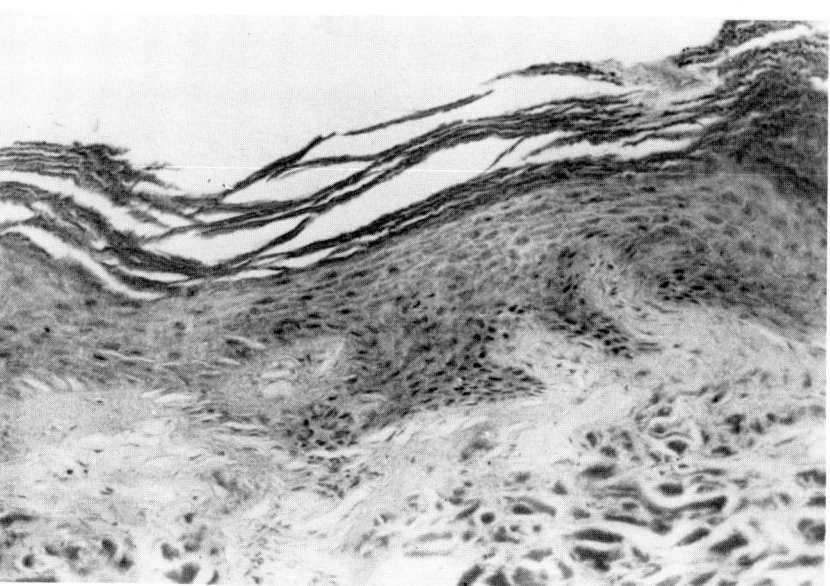

Fig 4.1 Many fungal hyphae are seen in the subcutaneous fat in this
section stained by the Periodic Acid Schiff method

Fig 4.2 Good preservation of the epidermal cell nuclei is present in
this section of skin stained with haematoxylin and eosin

4.3

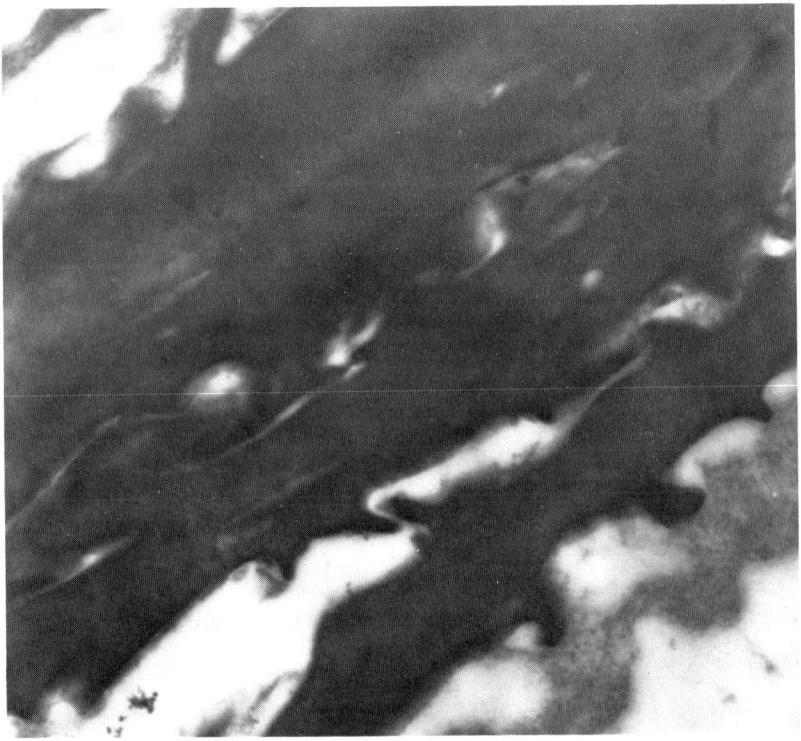

4.4

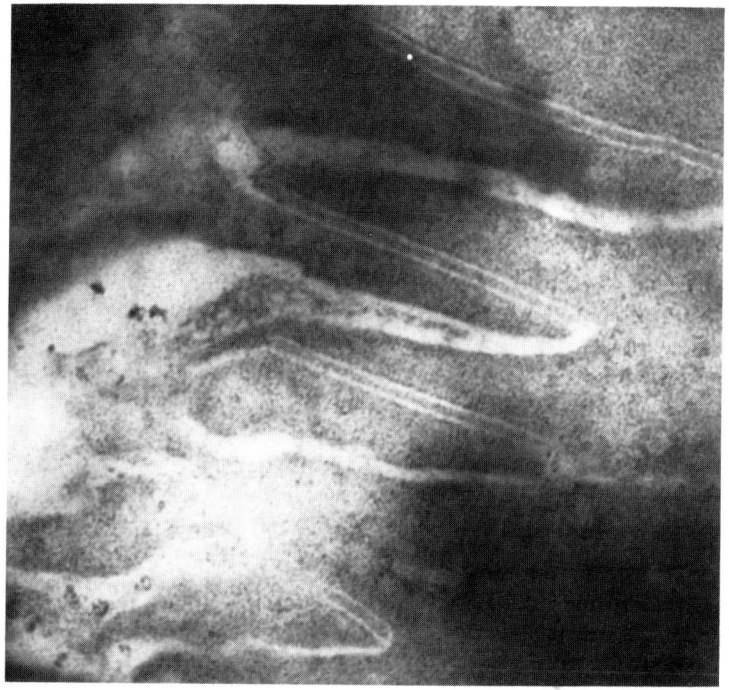

4.5

Fig 4.3 The cells of the epidermis which produce keratin
are stained selectively

Fig 4.4 Keratin magnified some 22,500 times under the electron microscope

Fig 4.5 Desmosomes are seen in this section of epidermis, magnified
with the electron microscope some 64,000 times

been described previously and were again prominent in the present
material (Fig. 4.1).

Despite all these problems, several examples of skin, including some
new material from Dr Verbov in Liverpool, have been examined and
found to have good histological preservation.

The outer keratinised layer, the epidermis and indeed the nuclei of
the epidermal cells were clearly visible (see Fig. 4.2). In mummified
tissues nuclear staining with haematoxylin has been found to be
unsatisfactory by several workers previously, presumably due to the
degradation of acidic radicles which are normally responsible for
satisfactory staining of nuclei. The connective tissue of the dermis
stained well with appropriate dyes although in some cases, the colour is
not what one expects, for instance, collagen fibres may stain red instead

of green with the Masson trichrome stain. Elastic fibres were demonstrated readily by the Verhoff stain and fat and voluntary muscle were
also seen. Sweat glands and blood vessels, the latter containing red and
white blood cells in the lumen were identified in the dermal connective
tissue.

Several immuno-histochemical stains have been tried and in particular the antikeratin labelled antibody was useful in staining selectively
those cells which produce keratin (see Fig. 4.3). Electron microscopy of
the skin was also carried out and preservation was such that many
elements could be identified. Keratin in the superficial layers was
prominent and rather shrunken nuclei were also seen (see Fig. 4.4).
Desmosomes with attached tonofilaments, features of keratin-
producing cells were present in some areas (see Fig. 4.5).

Intestine from Manchester mummies has proved interesting from
both the histological and histopathological points of view in the past.
Despite the fact that the intestine tends to undergo autolysis rapidly
after death, it has been shown previously that intestinal cells may be
demonstrated in mummified material and that these cells still contain
mucins which are capable of reacting with histochemical stains.
Moreover, an infestation with the worm *Strongyloides* was found in the
intestine of the mummy Asru. This is a parasite rather like *Bilharzia*, in
that the infection occurs when immature forms penetrate the skin from
infected water. Stagnant water is a particularly common source for both
these organisms and, not surprisingly, workers in flooded fields and
irrigation canals were and still are at risk.

More recently the material containing normal intestine has been
reviewed and immuno-histochemical stains applied. Of these the most
satisfactory was the antibody to the so-called carcino-embryonic antigen
(CEA). This substance, in addition to being found, as the name
suggests, in certain carcinomas and embryonic tissues, is also widespread throughout the intestine and it was extremely interesting that
CEA had persisted in mummified intestine and could be identified with
this technique (see Fig. 4.6).

Whilst the contents of the intestinal cells could be stained by
conventional methods nuclei could not be identified although their
probable site was indicated by rounded clear spaces in many of the
cells. It was with this in mind that the electron microscope was used to
examine material from histological blocks of the intestine. The photographs show that in fact the nuclei were present and whilst being

slightly shrunken appear to be well preserved at the electron optical level (see Fig. 4.7).

The brain, like the intestines, undergoes *post mortem* change rapidly after death. In addition, the ancient Egyptians tended to leave the brain to liquify for a few days before attempting to remove it and this, as might be expected, gives rise to additional problems for the histopathologist. However, much of the new brain material which has become available due to the endoscopic techniques has now been examined using the latest neuropathological staining methods and this has been quite fruitful. Whilst the individual cells and their nuclei could not be demonstrated, the many nerve fibres connecting the cells of the brain were recognised and blood vessels within the brain substance were seen (see Fig. 4.8). Histological sections have also been obtained from one of the cranial nerves (fifth) within the skull. The myelin sheaths of these nerve fibres could be seen and the remains of the nerve fibres within them. The membranes covering the brain (meninges) were also examined by histological methods and small calcified (Psammoma) bodies, a normal finding in the meninges, could be readily demonstrated.

In view of the fact that brain cells cannot be demonstrated with conventional stains, attempts have been made to use immunohistochemical techniques. Recently it has been demonstrated in fresh brains that glial cells, the connective tissue cells of the brain, contain a substance known as glial fibrillary protein (GFP). This can be used as a marker for these cells in both normal and neoplastic tissues. An antibody to GFP linked with dye is available and this has been used in several of the brain biopsies. Whilst the results were, to some extent, equivocal, it did appear that in some areas reactive GFP persists in the brain tissue from several mummies (see Fig. 4.9). This is certainly a method which warrants further consideration.

A striking feature in some of the brains was the peculiar *post mortem* change known as adipocere or, more popularly, grave-wax.[25] It was seen in two stages, the fully developed form consisting of masses of birefringent crystals in the tissues whilst in some of the biopsies adipocere was incompletely formed but could be stained with the periodic acid Schiff reagent. Adipocere formation is very familiar to forensic pathologists. It may occur in the tissues of any body which has remained hidden and hence allowed to undergo *post mortem* changes, particularly in damp surroundings. It is due to the hydrolysis of the

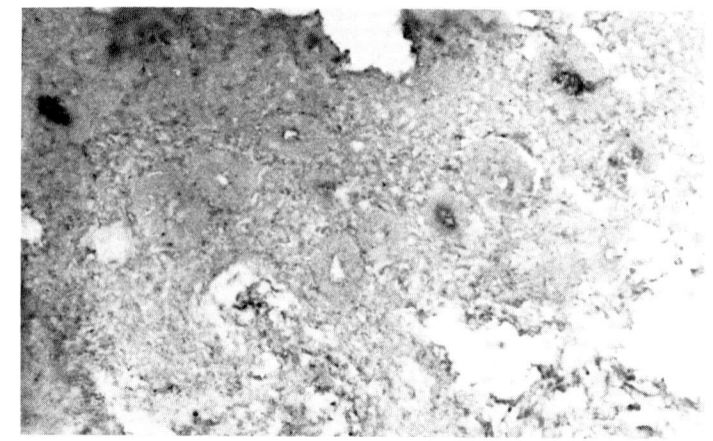

4.6

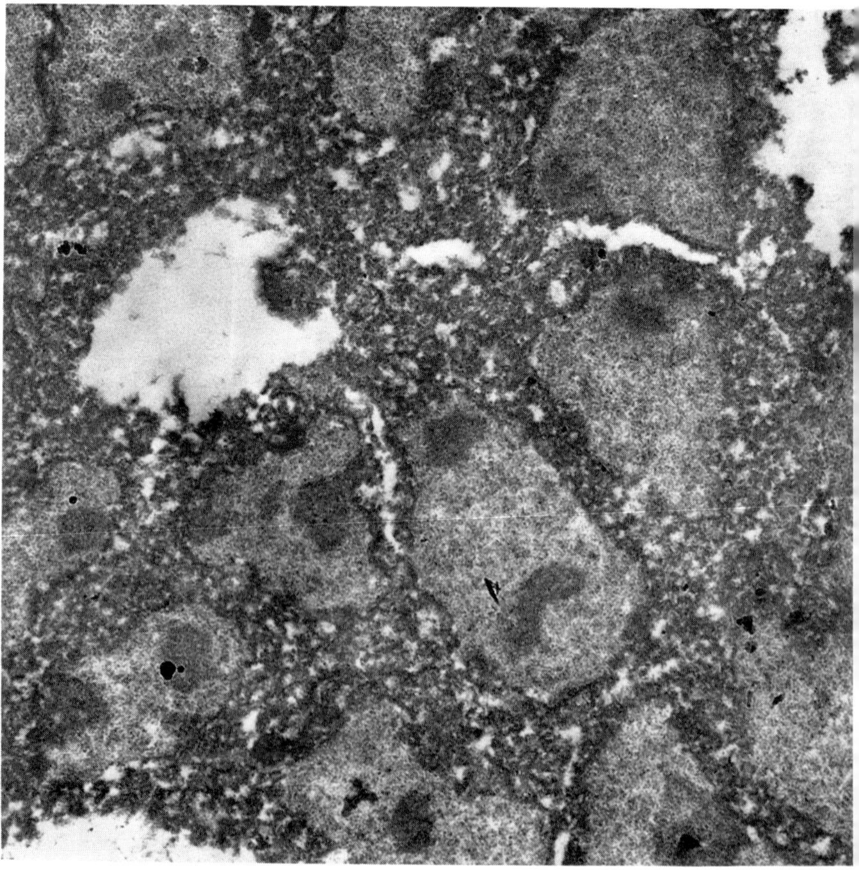

4.7

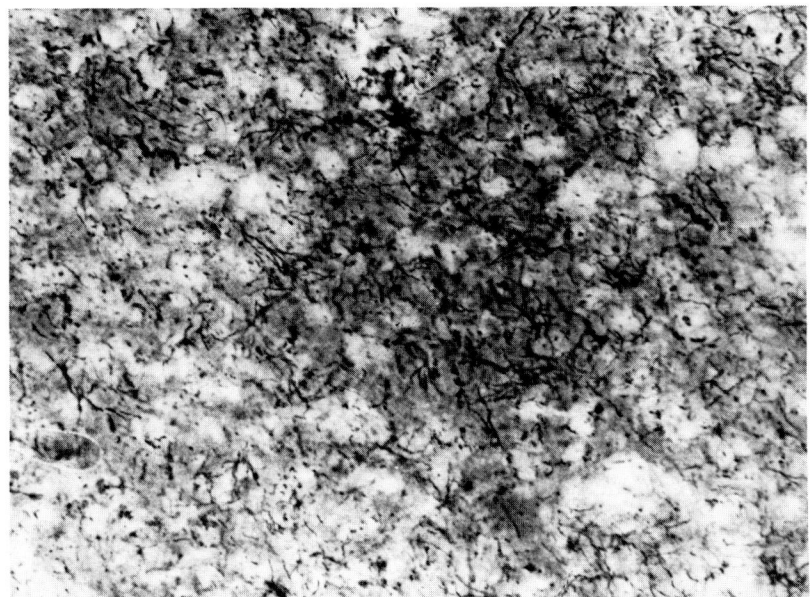

Fig 4.6 Carcinoembryonic antigen (CEA) is seen on the inner border of the glands in this section stained immunohistochemically with anti-CEA labelled antibody

Fig 4.7 The nuclei of the cells are seen quite clearly in this single gland multiplied some 10,500 times with the electron microscope

Fig 4.8 Nerve cells connecting the cells in the brain are seen in this section of brain impregnated by the Holmes silver method

neutral fats in the tissues to fatty acids and glycerol. The water necessary for hydrolysis may be taken out of the environment but more commonly it is extracted from the surrounding tissue and indeed, helps to preserve it in much the same way as natural or artificial mummification. By the very nature of mummification in ancient Egypt water was extracted from the tissues and the bodies were kept in dry surroundings. Hence, the water necessary for adipocere formation is not available and adipocere is seen only occasionally in Egyptian mummified tissue.[26] However, it is known that the brain was treated differently by the ancient Egyptians. The fact that they normally left it within the skull for a few days has received comment already. Moreover, endoscopy has also shown that in many instances they appear to have left a good deal of brain tissue behind. It would appear that this residual brain tissue had been allowed to undergo natural *post mortem* changes, hence the formation of adipocere.

Moving on to the histopathology of the brain, the most interesting find was in the biopsies of Mummy 22940, for in several samples of brain tissue there were the remains of the wall of a hydatid cyst. Heads (scolices) which, if allowed, would develop into new adult tape worms could be seen attached to the lining of the cyst and hooklets from these scolices could be demonstrated (see Fig. 4.10). Hydatid disease is caused by a tape worm called *Echinococcus granulosus*. Here, man is the intermediary host, the definitive host normally being a carnivorous animal such as the dog or wolf. Ova are discharged in the faeces of the animal and if these are ingested by man they develop into embryos in the duodenum. The embryos penetrate the wall of the duodenum and eventually may develop into hydatid cysts in practically any organ of the body. The cysts in some places may reach 20 cm in diameter and as they grow they develop pedunculated vesicles on the inside containing the scolices. By their continued expansion they produce an effect very much like that of a malignant tumour. Hence it is very likely that Mummy 22940 had severe headaches, gradual loss of vision and even fits before eventually lapsing into unconsciousness due to the increased intracranial pressure caused by the cyst increasing in size within a cranial cavity which is fixed in volume.

Prior to the use of endoscopy the only lung tissue available in Manchester was that found in one of the canopic jars belonging to the mummy Nekht Ankh. The lungs showed fibrous scarring and both histological and electron optical studies indicated that he was suffering from sand pneumoconiosis.[27] This condition is believed to be due to the inhalation of fine sand particles. It occurs in some desert populations and pathologically is closely allied to the silicosis which coal miners, quarrymen and stonemasons contract due to the inhalation of stone dust. It should not be confused with the presence of carbon pigment in the lung (anthrocosis) a condition which has been described in several mummies including Har-mose, ROM I and PUM II. Anthracosis is believed to be due to the inhalation of smoke arising from fires and oil

Fig 4.9 Foci of glial fibrillary protein (GFP) are seen in this section
of brain stained with anti-GFP labelled antibody

Fig 4.10 Part of the head of a developing tapeworm within a hydatid cyst
from the brain. The small dark structures are the hooklets which
attach the head to the inside of the cyst

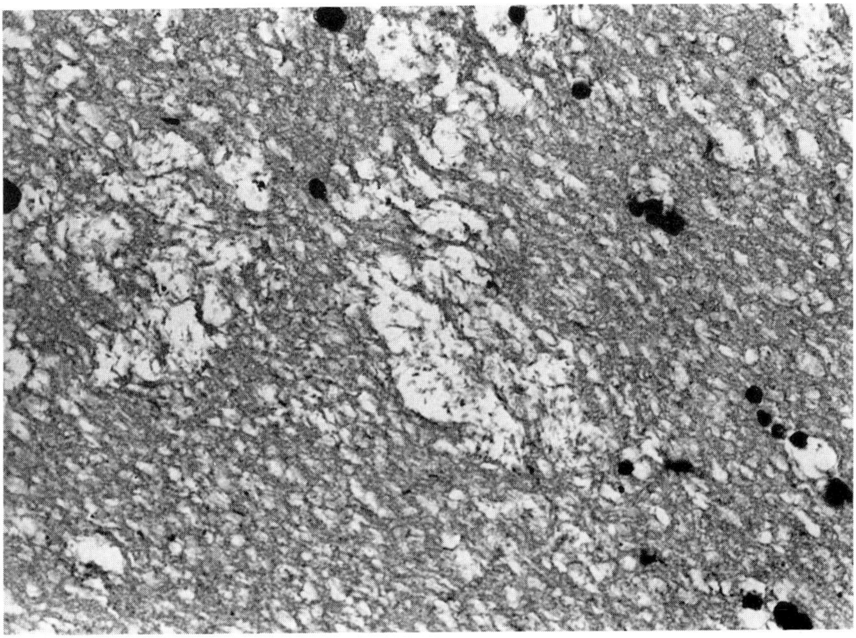

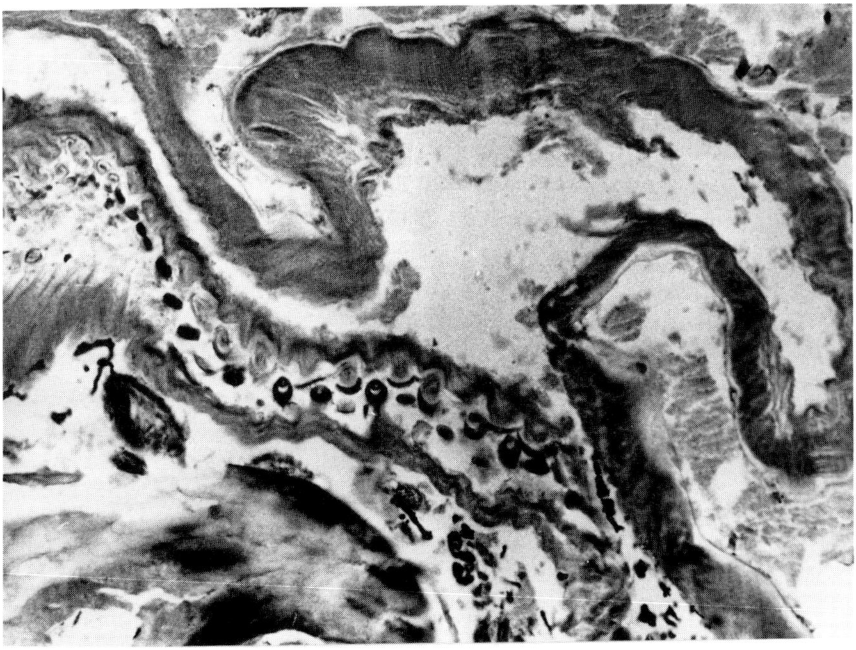

lamps which the ancient Egyptians used in small, poorly ventilated rooms.

Recently endoscopy has been carried out on the chest cavities of several mummies and small pieces of lung removed for study. Clear evidence of sand pneumoconiosis was seen in the lung biopsy from the mummy Khary. Similar changes have been reported in PUM II and it may well be that this condition was relatively common in Ancient Egypt. A further interesting find occurred in the lung biopsy from Asru. It will be remembered that this woman had been shown previously to be suffering from the worm infestation *Strongyloides*. The lung biopsy showed that she also had suffered from hydatid disease. There was clear evidence of the remains of a cyst in the lung and this was associated with fibrous and elastic tissue scarring in the adjacent lung tissue. The genesis of hydatid cysts has been described previously and from this it will be realised that as the larvae have to pass through the lungs before reaching other organs of the body, the lung is a common site for hydatid cysts to develop. Considering the small number of mummies examined, its presence in two of them suggests that this worm infestation may well have been a major problem in Ancient Egypt.

The diversity of the parasitic infestations in Egyptian mummies is quite staggering (see Table 1). It has been seen that all the Egyptian mummies examined by modern techniques as well as the head of 22940 showed evidence of some infestation and in two instances two or more parasites were involved in the same individual.

The methods by which these people became infected have been touched upon already and it only remains to stress how they appear to have come into contact with infected material at every turn. The problem is, of course, largely related to inadequate sanitation associated with total lack of appreciation of the cause of the diseases and how they

Table 1
Parasitic infections in five Egyptian mummies

PUM II	ROM I	1770	Asru	22940
Ascaris	Taenia Trichinella Bilharzia	Dracunculus	Strongyloides Ecchinococcus	Ecchinococcus

were transmitted. When they worked in the fields, flooded at the inundation, they were likely to have had their hands or feet penetrated by the *Bilharzia* or *Strongyloides* larvae. Unless their latrines were well away from their supply of drinking water, the latter would be contaminated and organisms such as *Ascaris* and *Dracuncula* likely to be ingested. Moreover, it has been seen that they were also at risk of developing the *Taenia* and *Trichinella* worms if they ate undercooked meat. Finally, they were even at risk when coming into contact with their domestic dogs, the latter probably being responsible for the *Ecchinococcus* infection of Asru and Mummy 22940. It was stressed in the opening paragraph of this chapter that finding the cause of a disease is an important stage before satisfactory specific treatment can be found, and although they did associate worms with disease,[28] all these parasitic infestations had to be dealt with by the ancient Egyptians with very little idea of their cause. Treatment was consequently empirical although it is quite possible that some of the antihelminthics such as pomegranate root, acacia leaves and juniper listed in the Ebers Papyrus for worm infestations may well have been effective.[29]

The other main disease which these studies have revealed is that of sand pneumoconiosis in the lungs. Here again, the ancient Egyptians were prisoners of their environment. They certainly had no way of escaping the fine clouds of dust blown up in sandstorms. Moreover, it may well be that they were at risk from contracting the closely related disease of silicosis whilst following their occupation. Certainly the dusty atmosphere in tombs must have resulted in some lung damage and of course the large number of stone masons who must have been involved in building all the fine monuments of ancient Egypt were also subjected to the same risk as modern stone masons. Little is known of how the ancient Egyptians coped with the increasing breathlessness and persistent cough which would result from these conditions. Interestingly enough, they realised that a cough could lead to a hernia, still very much a problem in modern times. They appeared to have had to be content with concentrating on treating the cough symptomatically, and certainly honey, which is mentioned as one treatment for a cough in the Ebers Papyrus, is still a popular constituent of modern cough medicine.[30]

[5]

BLOOD GROUPS IN ANCIENT EGYPT

In many cultures, blood has been believed to be of sacred and mystical significance. Blood sacrifice is known to have occurred in many ancient civilisations and stories of vampires stemming from the Middle Ages are well documented. Gladiators were encouraged to drink the blood of their fallen victims in the belief that it would give them strength. In contrast, although blood is mentioned many times in the Old Testament, the consumption of blood is expressly forbidden. This is the foundation for the refusal of present-day Jehovah's Witnesses to receive blood transfusions.

Even before the function of blood was clearly understood, abnormalities of the blood in the widest sense were thought to be the cause of many illnesses. Too much blood was held to be responsible for the evil humour that caused many chronic illnesses. Blood-letting, either by opening a vein or by the application of leeches, was practised for centuries and, indeed, still had advocates in the 1920s. The ancient Egyptians were aware of what they described as the 'heart over-filling with blood' but they did not appear to use bleeding as a therapy in humans. However, the veterinary section of the Kahun papyrus describes how oxen were treated by bleeding from the ear and tail.[1]

It is now appreciated, of course, that in many illnesses associated with blood disorders there is anaemia (a shortage of blood) rather than too much blood. As a result of this, those physicians who advocated blood letting succeeded only, in many cases, in making the patient's condition worse.

In physiological terms blood is necessary because all animal tissues require oxygen to carry out their metabolic function. The oxygen is carried by the haemoglobin in the red cells (erythrocytes) which acquires it from the air that we breathe into our lungs. Now, clearly, in order that blood can fill its role as an oxygen carrier it must travel throughout the body. Consequently, the first real understanding of the role of the heart and great vessels in the circulation of the blood came in 1616 when Harvey described the way in which the heart acted as a pump to propel blood throughout the body. It was soon recognised that the administration of blood into veins might well be beneficial to those people who had a decreased blood volume as a result of haemorrhage and it was only some fifty years after Harvey's discovery that experiments were published which showed that, in dogs at least, blood transfusions were possible, despite the difficult and necessarily primitive techniques involved. Moreover, early experiments seemed to show that blood could be transfused from sheep to man without mishap. Not surprisingly, however, in view of what we now know about the specificity of blood groups in man numerous deaths were also reported following attempted transfusion between animals and man and the technique fell into disrepute for a century or more.

However, a new stimulus for the investigation of the possibility of therapeutic blood transfusion in man came with Priestley's work on the discovery of oxygen and its role in respiration. In the light of these new discoveries the first serious attempts at transfusions between humans were reported in the 1820s by Blundell at Guy's Hospital in London.[2] The recipients were women who had had severe blood loss during childbirth. Although he was successful with some of his patients others had severe reactions and the work was not pursued further. In order to get over these difficulties other workers, seeking a substitute for blood to expand the blood volume after bleeding, used milk or salt solutions, and indeed saline in a physiological concentration is still a valuable short term substitute for blood in present medical practice.

The first major breakthrough, which eventually lead to the safe administration of blood, was the discovery of the ABO system of blood groups by Landsteiner in 1901.[3] It had been known for some years that mixing blood from different people would, in some instances, produce destruction (haemolysis) of some or all of the red blood cells. The haemolysins that destroyed the foreign cells were found to be naturally present in the serum of the blood. Landsteiner and later workers showed that there were four major blood groups: group A showed clumping (agglutination) with serum from group B individuals, while group B cells were agglutinated by group A serum. Some individuals whose cells were group O could not be agglutinated by either group A or group B serum, while the serum from group O people would agglutinate both A and B cells. There was a small number of people (group AB) whose cells could be agglutinated by both A and B serum but whose own serum appeared to be inert and did not react with either A or B cells. A summary of the characteristics of the four major blood groups is given in Table 2.

Since this discovery, numerous other antigens have been found on red cells and these are so complex that with the exception of identical twins it is very unlikely that any two people will have exactly the same combination of red cell antigens.

In the last thirty years, blood transfusion has become a safe and practical procedure. Patients logically receive blood which is of the same major blood group as their own. In practice, tests are carried out to ensure that the cells of the donor are compatible with the serum of the recipient. It has been estimated that without this compatibility testing, thirty percent of random transfusions would result in a severe haemolytic reaction – with a fatal outcome in some cases. Sometimes when testing the recipient's serum against a panel of cells, antibodies to blood group antigens other than the ABO system are found. These are not usually naturally occurring and tend to arise because of some prior immunisation with blood, perhaps as the result of a previous transfusion or pregnancy and childbirth.

In 1908 Ottenberg suggested that blood groups could be inherited.[4] This has proved to be correct and follows the classic Mendelian fashion. In its simplest form, each parent provides half the information (genes) necessary to determine the blood group of its offspring. If the gene for A or B is passed on, its presence is dominant with respect to O. An individual of group O occurs because neither parent has provided A or B genes, whilst someone of group AB will usually have received A from one parent and B from the other. A summary of the genes (genotype) possibly in each blood group (phenotype) is given in Table 3. From this it will be seen that an individual who is group A may have received a single or double dose of A from their parents. Another point worth noting is that it does not follow that the blood group of the offspring has to be the same as the parents, as the examples in Table 4 illustrate.

This kind of information about blood groups is important when one is attempting to trace relationships. At the present time, investigation of the main ABO blood groups, as well as many of the minor groups, is used extensively for evidence of paternity in affiliation proceedings. In

Table 2
Characteristics of four major blood groups

	Cells	Serum
Group	A	anti B
Group	B	anti A
Group	O	anti A + anti B
Group	AB	No isoagglutinins

Table 3
Genotypes of main blood groups

Phenotype	Genotype
Group O	00
Group A	AA ⎱ AO ⎰
Group B	BB ⎱ BO ⎰
Group AB	Group AB

this situation, however, the results can more reliably exclude, rather than confirm a putative father. With modern methods, paternity exclusions can achieve more than 99 percent accuracy.

The distribution of blood groups tends to vary in different races (Table 5). Evidence of different population distributions has been used to follow migrations and invasions. Information of this type is of particular relevance with regard to Egypt, since the Coptic Christians are assumed to be descended from the country's ancient inhabitants. In view of the religious and cultural differences which have tended to preserve their separate identity, one might expect to find that they have a characteristic blood group pattern when compared with the remainder of the population. However, whilst there appear to be differences in the distribution of blood groups between populations in the Delta when compared with southern Egypt, there do not appear to be significant differences in A and B gene frequencies between Coptic and Moslem Egyptians.[5] Clearly, more information concerning the distribution of blood groups amongst the ancient Egyptians might well be most valuable in explaining these findings.

Table 4
Influence of parental blood groups on child's blood group

Parent's genotype	AA × AA	AO × AO	AB × AB
Child's genotype	AA AA AA AA	AA AA OA OO	AA AB BA BB
Child's blood group	A A A A	A A A A	A AB AB B

Table 5
Blood group destruction in different countries

	United Kingdom %	North India %	South India %	Egypt %
Group A	37	38	19	33
B	8	19	26	24
AB	3	3	6	7
O	52	38	47	36

It has been suggested that the presence or absence of a particular blood group antigen confers advantages or disadvantages in survival. For instance, it is thought that the plague bacillus which ravaged Europe in the Middle Ages carried antigens similar to the blood group O. As individuals are less likely to produce antibodies against an antigen which is already present in their own bodies, people of group O were more prone to the plague. In contrast, those people not possessing the minor blood group called the Duffy antigen, most black West Africans, appear to be protected from a common type of malaria caused by the parasite *Plasmodium Vivax*. Other examples where blood groups are linked with disease concern group A individuals who have a higher incidence of gastric carcinoma than other blood groups, and those of group O who are more prone to stomach ulcers.

Returning, however, to ancient Egypt, a rather obvious drawback when it comes to determining the blood group of mummies is the absence of blood. Fortunately, ABO substances are found in tissues other than erythrocytes, and in some people blood group substances are also secreted in saliva and semen. This allows testing for blood groups to be done even in the absence of viable red blood cells and, in fact, most studies have been carried out on bone, muscle, mucosa or skin.

The first large survey of blood groups in ancient populations was done by Boyd and his colleagues in the 1930s.[6] Some three hundred mummies were tested, using mainly specimens of muscle, and a high incidence of group AB was found – the possible non-specific binding of anti-A and anti-B on to mummified tissue could have given rise to false positive results, hence a high incidence of group AB. This highlights the problem of interpretation of results, which still presents difficulty today.

Another problem for the investigator is that group A and B substances may degenerate with time and therefore failure of absorption leads to the false conclusion that the cases are group O. This was noted in particular by Candela in a study of ancient skeletons.[7] He pointed out that if the antisera was too strong, insufficient antibody absorption occurred and this might give an incorrect group O result.

Szulman[8] showed that the mucosa lining of the mouth, oesophagus and stomach gave strong reactions for A, B and HO antigens and consequently use of these tissues improves the chances of successful grouping.

Hart and his colleagues showed that the mummy Nakht was group B.[9] They tested specimens from the spleen and from one of the sinuses in the brain. In the latter they were fortunate to find intact red cells which were estimated to be at least three thousand years old, and these gave a positive result. Their experiments also demonstrated another pitfall for the serologist when the splenic material being tested proved to be heavily contaminated with bacteria. This contamination not only neutralised the anti-sera and so prevented a reaction but also destroyed the indicator cells.

Despite all these problems, a number of tests are available for the study of tissue from the Manchester mummies and are being investigated in Preston. There appears to be no 'best' test and it is intended to try a number and choose the one which seems to be the most suitable. Since blood is not available, most grouping is being carried out on muscle or bone. The tissue is pulverised with the aim of producing cell-free material. All systems are being carefully controlled and the results interpreted cautiously in view of the many variables which have been mentioned already.

One or more of the following tests are being used:

(1)   The agglutination inhibition reaction: this test relies on the

premise that antibody will be absorbed onto the surface of the cellular material being tested. This will result in a decrease in the strength of the anti-sera on subsequent testing against appropriate indicator cells. The test needs to be suitably controlled as some degree of non-specific absorption of human globulins may occur leading to misinterpretation of the results.

(2)   Mixed cell agglutination test: this procedure is also based on the fact that tissue cell surfaces containing blood group antigens are capable of capturing and retaining specific antibodies. However, in this system, instead of trying to detect a fall in antibody titre, the indicator cells added to the test will form visible rosettes when they attach to the appropriate antibodies. Once again, it is necessary to exclude any non-specific absorption of antibody. One control that has been used is a non-human serum produced by immunising rabbits with red blood cells from a sheep. The anti-sera thus produced can be used in parallel with the human anti-sera but using sheep erythrocytes as indicator cells.

(3)   Fluorescent antibody technique: this is related to the other tests in so far as specific antibodies are again absorbed on to appropriate tissues. Instead of indicator cells, the presence of the antibody is detected by fluorescent-labelled anti-human serum which attaches to the absorbed antibodies on the tissue cells. Since some tissues may have a natural fluorescence, it is again necessary to use strict controls to exclude any false positive results.

(4)   Serological micro-method: in this system, group O cells are incubated with mummified tissue. If A or B substances are present they will be absorbed on to the O cells. They can then be detected, using the appropriate anti-sera which will cause agglutination. If no agglutination occurs with anti-A or anti-B sera it may be because the tissue is group O and there is no A or B substance available to be absorbed onto the indicator cells. On the other hand, it may reflect deterioration of the A and B substances with time.

This last test has been used by Connolly and his co-workers to investigate the kinship between Smenkhkare and Tutankhamun.[10] Both mummies appeared to have the same blood group A2 and this, together with anthropological evidence, strongly suggested a close relationship between them.

Whilst the results of our own tests are not yet available for publication, it is hoped that the foregoing will have given the reader some insight as to the problems involved, as well as the enormous amount of information which may be gained concerning the relationships between both races and individuals in ancient Egypt, as well as the possible interrelationships between blood groups and the diseases from which the ancient Egyptians suffered.

[[6]]
DENTAL PROBLEMS DURING THE OLD KINGDOM – FACTS AND LEGENDS

After his visit to Egypt, Herodotus, the Greek traveller and historian of the fifth century BC, wrote of the status of the healing profession in that country in the following terms –

Medicine is practised among them on a plan of separation: each physician treats a single disorder and no more: thus the country swarms with medical practitioners, some undertaking to cure diseases of the eye, others of the head, others again of the teeth, others of the intestines, and some those which are not local.[1]

Unfortunately, he recorded no particulars of any kind of dental treatment. Whether treatment at the time was based on an understanding of cause and effect or fell into the category of spells, incantations and the use of empirical remedies is not known.

One fact that has emerged from the study of a limited selection of dentitions of the Ptolemaic period, which postdated the visit of Herodotus by three hundred years or more, is that many individuals, of adult and mature age groups, passed into their 'after life' with teeth affected by gross caries, attrition, apical abscesses and advanced alveolar bone disease.[2] Undoubtedly, then as now, some people had an inherent antipathy towards accepting treatment for the cure of any painful conditions and preferred to rely on hope, time and household remedies. Consequently, to generalise from the findings of a limited number of examples could lead to false conclusions. It is from the study of medical papyri and other literary sources that an understanding of the philosophy of their treatments will come, but it is from the study of paleodontology that knowledge of the success or otherwise of that treatment will arise. Other complementary sources of information can come from tomb and temple decorations, and the discovery of archaeological artefacts.

It is fortunate that considerable quantities of skeletal remains, recovered from tombs and cemeteries along the banks of the Nile, have retained their integrity. This, however, does not apply to those burials in the Delta, where the high water table is inimical to the preservation of any organic material. It is difficult to calculate the number of burials that have been made during the three thousand years of dynastic history and only an insignificant proportion of those has been recovered and recorded. Yet a consistent picture of dental ailments is gradually emerging.

Although comment on the teeth of the ancient Egyptians has been made for a considerable time, the significant study of paleodontology had its inception during the early decades of this century in the investigations of Elliot Smith and Wood Jones.[3] Valuable contribution was made by Ruffer and his associates,[4] and during the past twenty years illuminating studies have been conducted by scholars from Egypt, Europe and the United States. Extensive studies are still necessary before a comprehensive and conclusive picture emerges, but more than enough material already exists to provide a general survey of the subject.

The inhabitants of the Nile Valley can be divided into three social orders: Pharaohs, nobility and *fellahin*. There are examples of the dentitions of each in collections of human remains, housed in Egypt and in various museums and universities in America, England and other European countries.

It is a matter of regret that only single collections exist of the first two orders. The remains of the Pharaohs are those of the eighteenth dynasty, while those of the nobles are of the fourth dynasty. In spite of a lack of comparative material, it may be assumed that the general conclusions reached by the examination of these collections do provide an overall picture of the dental health and disease for the whole of the dynastic period. This, not only because we know that the dental history of the Pharaohs was a consistent one for some five hundred years, but also because the results of investigations of the dental conditions of the fellahin also show a consistency throughout the whole of the period. During the Ptolemaic period however, there seems to have been a dramatic increase in the incidence of caries. This could have resulted from the introduction of a cariogenic carbohydrate diet.

Pharaohs

With the exception of Tut'ankhamūn, who has not been removed from his rock-cut tomb in the Valley of the Kings, all the known royal mummies of the eighteenth dynasty have been collected together. When the priests of the twenty-first dynasty, *c.* 1100 BC, found many of the royal tombs in the Valley of the Kings pillaged and plundered, they collected together all the then known royal mummies. Those with disintegrated linen bandages were rewrapped, some were re-interred in the tomb of Amenophis II in the Valley of the Kings, whilst others were given a resting place in the tomb of Queen Inhapi, near to the village of Deir el-Bahri.

It was the disappearance of a kid from a herd of goats roaming in the Theban foothills that led to the discovery of these caches in 1881 AD. The mummies were eventually taken by members of the Department of Antiquities and housed in various etablishments, but all are now in the Egyptian Museum in Cairo.[5]

Elliot Smith had the privilege of making the first examination. He realised at the time the real value of a full radiological investigation, but had perforce to be content with a visual one.

The condition of the wrappings and the soft tissue covering of the mummies themselves varied considerably. It was only in those instances in which both had completely decayed and left bare the bony skeleton and teeth that Elliot Smith's observations were well founded. This is clearly illustrated by his conclusions regarding the dentition of Ramesses II. Finding the anterior teeth clean and in an excellent state of preservation, he concluded, certainly with some misgivings, that this condition was typical of the remainder of the dentition.[6] Nothing could have been further from the truth. This was established when a radiological examination was made by the Michigan University expedition. The findings revealed a dentition with extreme wear of all the posterior teeth, many with the pulp chamber exposed, apical abscesses, and advanced alveolar bone disease.[7] These observations were later confirmed when the mummy was taken to France for preservation and, in May 1977, subjected to gamma ray irradiation.[8] The radiographs taken at that time, revealed not only the dental sepsis, but also a large area of osteomyelitis of the mandible. It is therefore possible that the Pharaoh's life expectancy was shortened by a general septicemia initiated by gross dental sepsis.

The mummy of Amenophis III had undergone considerable damage and deterioration, a combination of the work of the tomb plunderers and of the ravages of time. Thus Elliot Smith was able to give an accurate and vivid picture of the Pharaoh's sufferings caused by severe dental caries, apical abscesses and advanced alveolar bone disease. It was this description, together with an unreconcilable statement about the existence of an organised dental profession, that inspired the investigation, some two decades ago, of the dental health of the ancient Egyptians, and the testing of the veracity of some conflicting statements.

Although Elliot Smith's work had been of inestimable value and has been the definitive contribution on the subject for more than half a century, it has now been superseded by the sterling investigations by the Michigan University expedition. This expedition, in conjunction with the University of Alexandria, carried out complete radiological surveys of the royal mummies during the seasons of 1967 to 1975 and these were concluded in 1978.

During the first season, a radioactive isotope, ytterbium-169, was used as the source of energy to expose x-ray film. As the mummies rested within an oak casket covered with a leaded glass case, the film had perforce to be placed along the distant side of these containers. In spite of this, valuable and interesting data resulted. There were deficiencies and drawbacks to the technique, however, and these inspired the development of other types of equipment. During the next and following seasons, a General Electric 90 kV dental unit was specially adapted and used, with uniformly consistent results.

With the use of this type of equipment, the museum authorities allowed the removal of the glass covering of the wooden casket, so that it became possible to place the x-ray cassette adjacent to the head of the mummy. Thus the resulting skeletal radiograph could be marred only by the opacity of the linen wrappings of the mummy and any detail arising from the rays passing through one $1\frac{1}{2}$ inch board.

Following his interpretation of the lateral projection radiographs of the crania, James E. Harris, the leader of the expedition, summarised his findings –

The pharaohs and queens of the New Kingdom – a period of almost 500 years – were heterogeneous from the view point of facile profile and dental occlusion. Most of these rulers suffered from periodontal disease and attrition, where the degree of severity was associated with the chronologic age of the given individual. Except for the very old, most of these mummies had their full complement of teeth, including third molars. In old age, the dentition demonstrated severe wear, with the exposure of the pulp chamber and periapical abscesses as well as periodontal loss of the supporting alveolar bone. Dental caries or decay did not seem to be significant in this group.

As previously stated, the mummy of Tut'ankhamūn still remains in his tomb in the Valley of the Kings. During Howard Carter's examination and restoration of the contents, an opportunity was afforded to Derry to unwrap the linen bandages covering the mummy and to conduct a visual inspection of it. Although the lips were apart and the anterior teeth could be assessed, Derry confined his observations of the teeth to the following paragraph: 'The upper and lower wisdom teeth had just erupted the gum and reached to about half the height of the second molar. Those on the left side were not so easily seen but appeared to be in the same stage of eruption.'[9]

In an attempt to prove family relationship of the two pharaohs, Smenkhkare and Tut'ankhamūn, Harrison, Abdullah and Leek were granted permission by the Egyptian Department of Antiquities to examine the mummy of Tut'ankhamūn. Prior to the visit in 1968, information concerning the electricity supply to the tomb was unobtainable, nor was it known how the examination could be conducted. Another unknown factor was the availability of a portable x-ray machine. Consequently, with the aid of the research staff at the Atomic Energy Authority, Harwell, a technique was perfected of taking panoramic radiographs of a mummy's dentition, using as the source of energy the radioactive isotope Iodine[125]. This proved an ideal technique, giving excellent detail of both teeth and alveolar bone. The long exposure of three hours could be a disadvantage for multiple use but no drawback for a single one.[10]

The members of the Egyptian Antiquities Department expressed enthusiasm for the project, but when on inspection of the royal mummy, a thin layer of highly polished resin was found beneath the Pharaoh's chin, permission to penetrate it with a sharp needle of less than 1 mm in diameter, with the isotope encapsulated in its head, was withdrawn. Permission, however, was granted to use the isotope but as it was not possible to place the head of the needle in the optimum position, the resulting panoramic radiograph proved to be a disappointment.[11] All was not lost, though, because it was possible to obtain and use a portable x-ray machine in the tomb. A lateral projection of the skull was taken and the film successfully developed in an improvised darkroom in a bedroom of the Old Winter Palace Hotel. As with all lateral projections of the skull, much detail is lost of both teeth and alveolar bone. Nevertheless the radiograph revealed a complete dentition, with very little wear of the occlusal surfaces of the teeth. No caries or alveolar bone disease could be detected and, as Derry had observed, the third molars were partially erupted.

The nobility

The skeletal remains recovered from Cheops' western necropolis represent the most important collection of human remains of the ruling classes of ancient Egypt. The cemetery is contemporary with the Great Pyramid (*c.* 2650 BC) and in it were buried Cheops' queens, royal descendants, high priests and court officials. This material was recovered during the excavation of the *mastaba* tombs which took place during the first four decades of this century.

Two expeditions were principally involved, one organised by the Akademie der Wissenschaften, Vienna and the Roemer-Pelizaeus Museum, Hildesheim, under the direction of Hermann Junker,[12] the other by Harvard University and the Boston Museum of Fine Arts, and led by George Reisner.[13]

The bodies had been buried in wooden coffins in a recess situated at the bottom of a rock-hewn shaft some thirty feet below the superimposed *mastaba* chapels and offering rooms. Although approximately 4,500 years old, many skeletons had retained their integrity, but others, due to the collapse of the wooden coffin, and sometimes to stone falling from the roof of the recess, were in various stages of disintegration. The collection of crania recovered by Junker is now housed in the Anthropologische Abteilung, Naturhistorisches Museum, Vienna. These crania were subjected to a critical appraisal during 1969 and the results published (JEA LXVI).

The members of the Manchester Museum Mummy Project are always interested in comparative material. Realising the outstanding importance of Reisner's collection, both for its own sake and also for comparative purposes, it was decided that an application be made to the Egyptian Department of Antiquities for a concession to examine it. No information was forthcoming from any of Reisner's published works concerning the condition or the amount of material recovered, nor could any information be gained from Egypt, except that it was kept in a 'bones magazine' situated on the desert some distance from the Great Pyramid. Nevertheless it was decided to make an investigation and ascertain the desirability of making a complete survey.

When admittance to the storehouse was eventually gained, there, along a wall of the chamber, were 166 wooden boxes. Some were in a good state of preservation, but others had suffered damage caused by the enormous fluctuations of desert temperatures. In each one, carefully laid and meticulously packed on a bed of chaff and straw had been the bones recovered from a single burial. There were two tables covered with crania and a few mandibles, whilst on the floor beneath the tables and strewn around, were a number of wicker baskets containing mandibles, and post cranial skeletal material. A preliminery survey was made, and the results subsequently published (Z.Ä.S. CX1, 1, 1984).

The results of the investigation were so encouraging that the

Fig 6.1 Part of the storehouse or 'Bones Magazine' showing some of the dry skulls of members of Cheops' court. On the lower right are wicker baskets filled with a miscellaneous collection of bones

members of the Manchester Museum Mummy Project decided that, if arrangements could be made, a full-scale examination should be made. Accordingly on behalf of the Director of Manchester Museum, the curator of the Egyptian Department applied for a further concession to Dr Ahmed Kadri, Chairman of the Egyptian Antiquities Organisation.

Permission was duly granted, and the following description of the dentition of these nobles forms a part of the full report of the investigation.

By utilising the distinguishing features used by anatomists for identification of sex and age, it was possible to divide the collection of 118 skulls as follows:

Table 6

Age	20–24	25–34	35–44	senior	Total
Male	3	52	8	0	63
Female	10	20	6	2	38

In addition there were fourteen adolescent and three juvenile skulls. None of the mandibles in the collection were united with their maxillas, and no help could be gained from the archaeologist's identification mark, in the endeavour to unite the two jaws. Using the articulation of the teeth, it was possible to unite some, but the task was so time-devouring that it was not pursued. Determination of sex rests on the shape of the arch, size of teeth, and muscle marking of the bone.[14]

Examination of the dentitions showed that the following numbers of teeth were present. The figure in parenthesis shows the possible total.

Table 7

	Male	Female	Adolescent	Juvenile
Maxilla	560 (1008)	328 (608)	80 (196)	17 (36)
Mandible	360 (752)	184 (496)	61 (140)	26 (36)

Each lost tooth leaves a characteristic pattern in the supporting alveolar bone, so characteristic that the only possibility of a diagnostic error is when a tooth has been removed immediately before death. If a tooth is removed *ante mortem*, the alveolar bone is not diseased, and healing is normal, the alveolar bone assumes a distinctive pattern. If, however, the alveolar bone was diseased, a different shape results. Should a tooth be lost as the result of injury or violence, again an unmistakable pattern is presented.

Two factors are mainly responsible for the *post mortem* loss of teeth:

(1) The organic elastic fibres of the periodontal membrane which attaches the tooth to its socket, gradually disappears, thus all conical rooted teeth, which includes incisors and some premolars, are at risk.

(2) The thin covering of alveolar bone enveloping the roots becomes extremely fragile, easily damaged and fractured, thus allowing the tooth to fall from its socket.

With regard to dental hygiene, the clean and polished appearance of most teeth showed that these people practised dental hygiene of a high

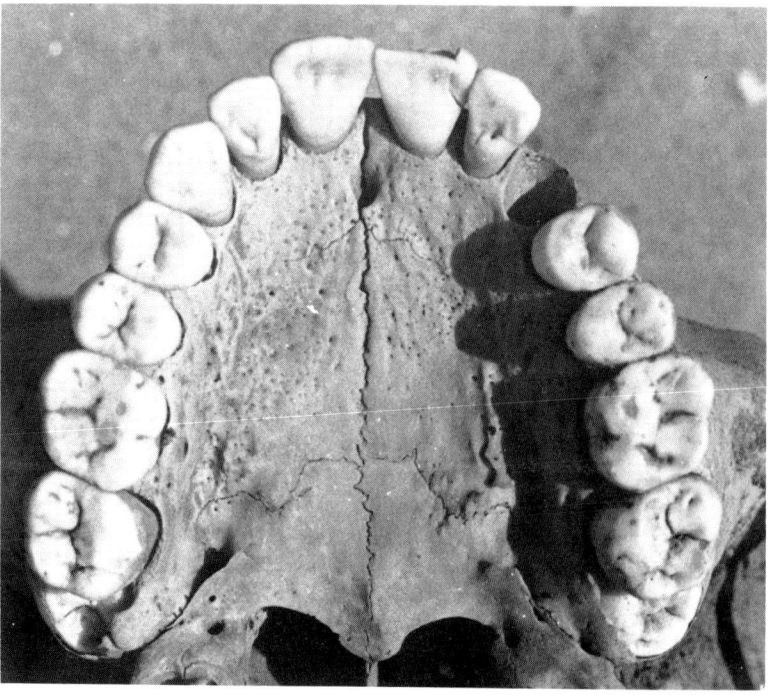

Fig 6.2 An atypical adolescent dentition, showing no wear on the cusps except those of the first molars. The canine missing from the dentition was lost *post mortem*

standard. In many isolated communities in Africa, it is a common experience to see individuals cleaning and polishing their teeth with the aid of a frayed end of a twig. Probably this or another similar system was used. Fortunately the movement of the saliva-moistened tongue is enough to prevent accumulation of tartar except around the lingual necks of the lower teeth. Here the mastication of a fibrous diet helps to minimise the accumulation.

Only thirty-eight carious cavities were found in 1,188 teeth, which represents 3.19 percent. Some of these were pit cavities, others were confined to a single surface, whilst in only a small minority had the decay invaded two surfaces. In only one instance had the caries progressed to invade the pulp chamber.

There is a possibility that some of the missing teeth from the dentitions could have been carious. As the majority of these were the self-cleansing front teeth, however, which are not so liable to be attacked by caries, the true percentage of carious teeth could well be lower.

No hypoplastic teeth were seen and the larger proportion of caries seen in male dentitions can be accounted for by the heavier chewing power of the male. All male dentitions of each different age group show a greater degree of wear on the cusps of the teeth, which increases the

Table 8
Carious cavities

| | Male | | | |
| | Maxilla | | Mandible | |
Age group	No. affected	Cavities	No. affected	Cavities
20–24	1	1	1	1
25–34	10	15	3	4
35–44	1	2	1	1
	Female			
20–24	2	3	0	0
25–34	2	2	5	6
35–44	0	0	1	2
	Juvenile and adolescent			
	Maxilla		Mandible	
Age group	No. affected	Cavities	No. affected	Cavities
0–19	0	0	1	1
Total	16	23	12	15

liability of fracture of the enamel, thus creating stagnation areas. At the same time the heavier chewing pattern increases the chances of food-packing between the molar teeth. These are all significant factors in the development of caries.

Wear of the cusps of the teeth so characterises almost every dentition that it could be described as universal. It is seen on the cusps of deciduous teeth, in the permanent molars of juvenile dentitions, and it progressed unremittingly throughout life.

During the early stages the pattern of wear can be described as horizontal, but as wear persisted and the mandibular joint undertook wider excursions during mastication, the pattern changed. The wear on the occlusal surfaces of the upper teeth was greater on the occlusal-palatal side, whilst in the lower arch the wear pattern was in the reverse direction. This applies principally to the chewing teeth; when the incisor teeth were worn, the reduction was then mainly horizontal.

It is indeed fortunate that the dental pulp responds to the stimuli produced by the irritation arising from the constant abrasion, and deposits secondary dentine within the pulp chamber while at the same time its vessels retreat away from the area of destruction. Otherwise

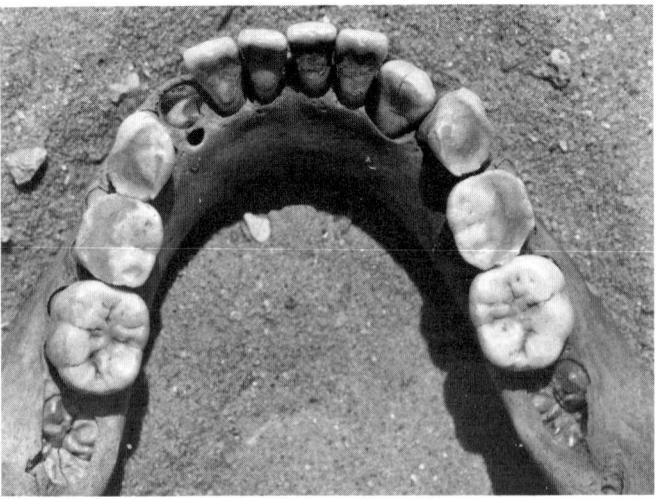

Fig 6.3 Juvenile dentition, age 10–11. There is marked attrition on the deciduous molars and the buccal cusps of the permanent molars are already worn

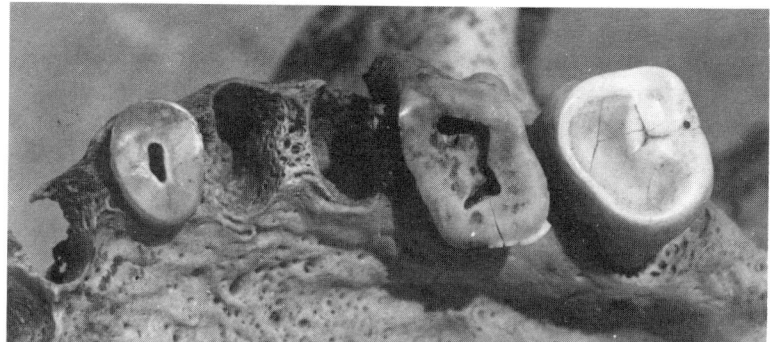

.4

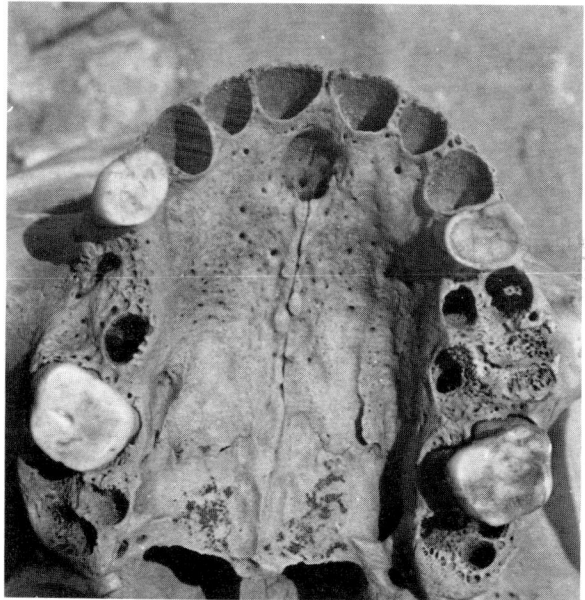

6.5

Fig 6.4 Attrition on the canine and molar resulted in exposure of the pulp chambers. The subsequent infection led to extensive apical alveolar bone destruction

Fig 6.5 The abscesses arising from the palatal roots of both upper first molars penetrated into the Antrum of Highmore. The teeth were eventually exfoliated, providing a much needed drainage path. All the anterior teeth were lost *post mortem*

every adult individual would have suffered from multiple abscesses. In those instances where the rate of wear overtakes that of the deposition of secondary dentine, the resulting exposure of the pulp chamber allows the ingress of pathological organisms. This is followed by a painful inflammation of the vessels and their eventual necrosis. During this period the organisms multiply and invade the periapical tissues, and this results in abscess formation and swelling of the surrounding tissues. Twenty-nine male dentitions exhibited seventy-two apical abscesses and twelve female dentitions exhibited forty-five apical abscesses.

These numbers represented those abscesses in which the pus made an escape route through the palatal or buccal alveolar plate. If it had been possible to radiograph each specimen, the number revealed would have been greater. Some abscesses remain confined to the body of the alveolar bone whilst others, especially those that arise from the palatal root of an upper molar, invade the Antrum of Highmore. This would be an unfortunate complication, as even today, this painful condition can be cured only by a complicated surgical operation. There are two other types of abscesses associated with the teeth of these individuals, each having a different aetiology and they will receive comment later.

Tartar is the result of a deposition of calcium salts from the saliva. These consist mainly of calcium phosphate with small and varying amounts of magnesium and carbonate. Tartar usually accumulates in the region of the orifices of the various salivary ducts, i.e. the lingual surfaces of the lower incisors and the buccal surfaces of the upper teeth. It is initially soft, but hardens and becomes darker the longer it remains *in situ*. By using the signs produced by these changes, it was found that there were examples arising from the following causes:

(1) faulty hygiene,
(2) accumulations occurring during a terminal illness;
(3) painful conditions of the periodontal membrane or the surrounding soft tissues discouraging dental hygiene;
(4) lack of mastication;
(5) stagnation areas produced by the *ante mortem* loss or absence of opposing teeth.

Some twenty-eight third molar teeth were absent from thirteen male and five female dentitions. In a few instances this was due to eruption failure, but development failure of the tooth germ itself was the cause in the majority of cases. Examination of other collections has shown instances of one, two, three and four third molars absent from the dentition.

A double mesio-angular impaction was seen in a female dentition and a similarly positioned single impaction in a male dentition. Both individuals had died before the abnormality had an opportunity to give rise to any symptoms.

This was not so in five other instances where the normal vertical eruption of the tooth had given rise to an osteomyelitis in the surrounding alveolar bone. This would have been preceded by an inflammation of the surrounding soft tissues, and trismus, i.e. an inability to open the mouth. Other complications at the time could have been a diffuse cellulitis and Ludwig's angina, both conditions that can be resistant to surgical and antibiotic treatment and at times have fatal consequences.[15]

The pathological changes seen in the supporting structures of the teeth were varied and the aetiology often confused, because of the conjunction of two or more pathological conditions. However the areas affected can be summarised as follows:

Margins Small triangular serrations would arise as the result of an inflammation involving the gingival crevasse, and this would be followed by a destruction of the junction of the epithelium and enamel cuticle. This would cause the alveolar bone and periodontal membrane to be exposed to an invasion of bacteria. Many factors can be responsible for such a condition, but neglected oral hygiene is the most common.

Pin-like pitting seen on the cervical end of the alveolar bone is most probably the result of a hypoplastic gingivitis. Nasal obstruction, incompetent lip seal, pregnancy and vitamin deficiency are among some of the predisposing factors of this condition.

Interdental bone destruction Gross resorption of the interdental septum which results in a crater-like depression, can be caused by one or a combination of different factors. Each, however, is associated with a chronic gum disease. It is preceded by the loss of the ginvigal papillae, and this would encourage food retention and packing. When this is the principal aetiological factor, it is the teeth in the buccal segment that are at greatest risk. This area and the bifurcation of the roots of molar teeth are the common sites for the beginning of a periodontal abscess. Infection and absorption of the surrounding alveolar bone can be

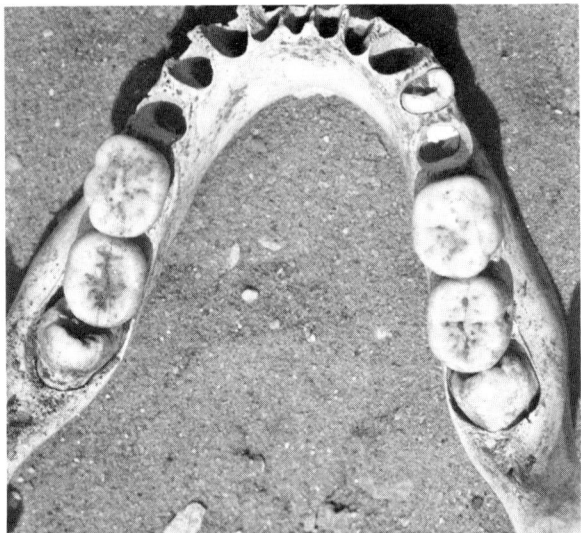

6.6

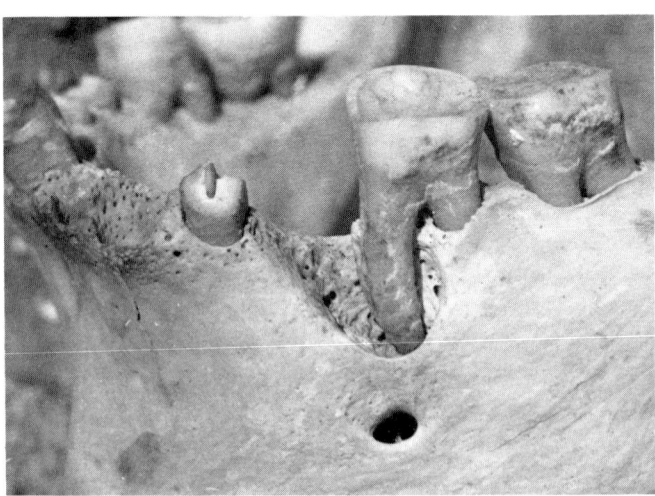

6.7

Fig 6.6 Adolescent dentition, age 15–16. Both third molars show a
mesio-angular impaction, but death intervened before any painful symptoms
arose. The cusps of the first molars are already worn flat

Fig 6.7 The abscess involving the mesial root of the molar probably arose from
an infection of the periodontal membrane caused by food retention. This would
have facilitated the loss of the more anterior tooth

extensive but also at times can be confined to a deep narrow pocket. In one male mandible, the whole of the mesial septum of a first molar had been absorbed away.

Periapical   This involves the loss of an area of the outer plate of the alveolar bone in the region of the apical end of the tooth. In its early stages it is small and confined and is sometimes given the name 'fenestration'. In its later stages the whole of the buccal surface of the root can be denuded of its bony support. The condition must not be confused with a sinus, which is the escape route of pus arising from an apical abscess. The condition is the result of a changing occlusal pattern brought about by the wear of the dental cusps. Instead of the stresses and strains produced during mastication being borne evenly along the whole of the root surface, they are transferred along the surface of the root at an angle. The pressures become centralised at the apex of the tooth, then transmitted to the enveloping bone, the cells of which eventually become inflamed and the outcome is an osteonecrosis of the area.

General

(1)   A continuation of the factors which produce a chronic gingivitis will eventually cause extensive destruction of the tooth's supporting structures. In some instances, the end result is a complete absorption of the alveolar bone, leaving the palate and the mandible quite flat and without any sign of a ridge.

(2)   A bacterial infection of the cancellous cells of the alveolar bone can result in an osteomyelitis, characterised externally by sieve-like holes in the cortex of the bone. These can be discrete or coalesced, circumscribed or occupying a diffuse area. The condition can arise following the necrosis of the dental pulp or from an infection of the periosteum. In the latter instance an infection of the surrounding tissues of an erupting third molar can be the cause. It is also possible that some of the *cures* used by these individuals in the hope of alleviating painful symptoms, could have been responsible for the infection.

Whilst there were examples of each one of the foregoing pathological changes in the alveolar bone, 38.09 percent of male and 73.68 percent of female maxillas were free of any type of disease. Marginal degeneration, often incipient, was seen in 34.65 percent of the crania, and

Fig 6.8 Osteomyelitis of the maxilla caused the sieve-like perforations in the palate, whilst the bridge of bone was the result of the action of apical abscesses. The abscess arising from the palatal root emerged on to the palate whilst the abscesses on the buccal apices made a pathway through the buccal plate

amongst those included were juveniles and young adults. In these cases the condition was regarded as a symptom of a chronic gingivitis acquired during a period of ill health or during a terminal illness.

Attrition of the dental cusps was the principal factor primarily responsible for the most serious breakdown of the bony tissues. Its action followed two completely different paths. The initial one was the necrosis of the dental pulp, and the subsequent apical abscess which often caused a cavernous destruction of the enveloping bone. The other was the traumatic occlusion resulting from the change in cuspal pattern. The abnormal stresses and strains produced by mastication were inimical to the life of the cells of the surrounding alveolar bone. A gingivitis, followed by a breakdown of the bony tissues, could leave the tooth devoid of any support.

The pathological changes observed in the mandibular bone were considerably less than in the maxilla, as the dense calcified nature of the mandible is more resistant to the strains imposed upon it.

Five apical abscesses were observed arising from discoloured incisor teeth. The discoloration is usually symptomatic of the rupture of the apical vessels, the result of a sharp blow on the tooth. In one instance, a male, the apical abscess from one lower incisor drained into the buccal

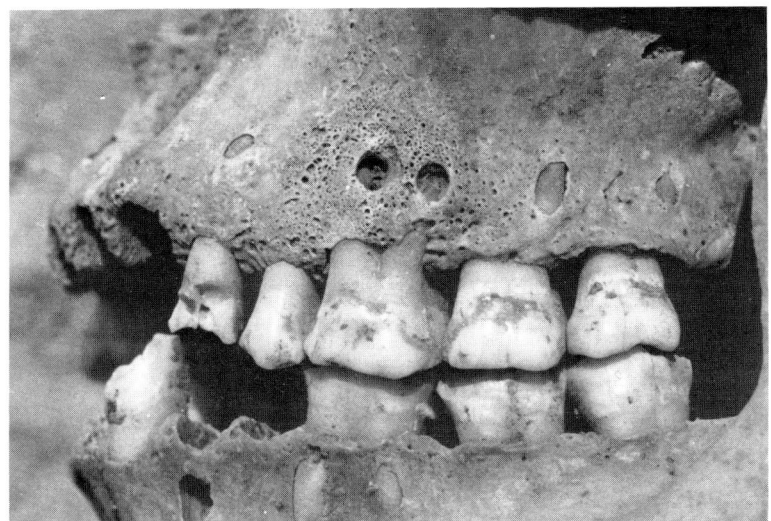

6.9

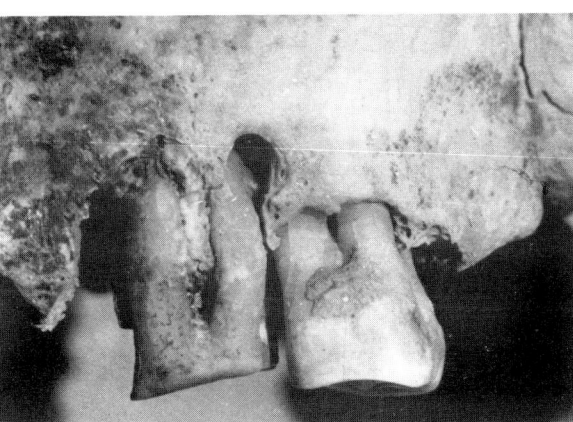

6.10

Fig 6.9 The apical abscesses from the buccal roots of the first upper molar have made an escape route through two circular and symmetrical sinuses. The sieve-like appearance of the surrounding bone is the result of osteomyelitis. The roots of the other two molar teeth are partially denuded of alveolar bone, the result of abnormal root pressures caused by traumatic occlusion

Fig 6.10 An apical abscess on the distal root of the upper first molar made an exit through the buccal plate. A periodontal abscess has denuded the mesial root of all the adjacent bone and traumatic occlusion was responsible for the complete loss of the alveolar bone covering the buccal surfaces of the two roots

sulcus, whilst that from the other incisor made an escape route through the lingual alveolar plate.

A central incisor of a female mandible was missing from the dentition. As the two adjacent teeth were standing at an angle inclined towards one another, the tooth had most probably been knocked out of its socket some time previously, the result of an accident or injury.

Two individuals had suffered severe damage to the premaxilla and incisor teeth. In both instances the teeth and the outer plate of alveolar bone were missing. Healing of the bone and a collapse of the buccal segments showed that the injuries were *ante mortem*, and had not proved fatal. It is impossible to estimate the amount of the damage to the soft tissue covering of the face, but the disfigurement would have been considerable.

Pitting of the bony palate indicative of an inflammatory mucosa was observed on two occasions, and also on many palates were small sharp wave crests of bone in the molar region, probably the result of an inflammation of the soft tissue covering. No suggestion can be made as to whether this condition arose from the individual's efforts to alleviate pain, the chewing of masticatories or other causes.

No cleft or other deformities were observed.

Almost every dentition was situated within well developed arches. Two juvenile dentitions presented a palatal deflection of the maxillary incisors. Such an irregularity could result from a habit, indulged in from an early age, of lying in a prone position on a firm bundle placed beneath the lower third of the face. Such a habit could be a family trait, but no support for this hypothesis could be gained from the archaeologist's identification number.

Crowding of the mandibular teeth in the buccal segment was recorded in two cases, probably as a result of pressure from the habit of resting the face on the palm of the hand.

One female dentition presented proclinated upper incisors indicative of a thumb-sucking habit.

In two mandibles, the second deciduous molars were retained in the permanent dentition. As it was not possible to radiograph the specimens, it is not known whether the permanent premolars were impacted or congenitally absent.

To summarise, only one individual could have suffered the pangs of toothache caused by a decayed tooth, but many individuals of mature age knew of the pain, swelling and malaise associated with an alveolar abscess. A high standard of dental hygiene was practised and no pathological conditions were seen apart from the results of a mild gingivitis, in the dentitions of those individuals whose death occurred before they were twenty-five years of age. Attrition of the cusps in the older age groups gave rise to considerable disease, via the necrosed dental pulp and by causing the degeneration of the supporting bony structures. Instances of osteomyelitis superimposed on other pathological conditions gave the impression that their pharmacopoeia sometimes failed to realise their expectations. All in all, those who died before the age of twenty-five years had good dentitions. Those who lived longer suffered from the constant progression of any dental disease acquired during life.

The conviction was gradually formed during the examination of many collections of dry skulls that the ancient Egyptians failed to equate the swelling of the soft tissues of the face caused by an acute alveolar abscess, and the pain associated with any kind of dental disease, with its causative factor i.e. a diseased tooth. Had they done so, a technique would have been quickly developed to remove the offending unit, and this would, in most instances, have been accomplished with extreme ease. If the foregoing premise is wrong, then the answer must lie in their psychology and their philosophical attitude towards the events of life.

Fellahin [the peasants]

The human remains from many cemeteries along the Nile Valley have been investigated by a number of paleopathologists since the beginning of the century. Amongst those who have made a major contribution to our knowledge of the dental health and disease of the teeth of the fellahin include: Armelagos (America); Strouhal (Czechoslovakia); Alexandersen (Denmark); Batawi (Egypt); Wood Jones, Elliot Smith, Ruffer (England); Quenouille (France); Nielsen (Sweden).

An almost consistent picture of the condition of the teeth is presented. It is not proposed to particularise each investigation, but to give illuminating summaries presented by three investigators –

Elliot Smith concluded his observations as follows:

Both in Nubia and Egypt the ordinary form of dental caries is extremely rare in Predynastic and Protodynastic people, and among the poorer classes it never became common until modern times. But as these people ate coarse food, mixed with a considerable amount of sand, the teeth rapidly wore down and as a result the pulp cavities became opened up: in the fertile soil of the exposed dental pulp, septic infection found a much readier place to attack than the hard resisting enamel and dentine that the tooth itself afforded; hence it is common to find alveolar abscesses without dental caries. Most of the dental disease of the archaic Egyptians and the poorer classes of Ancient Nubians in all periods is to be explained this way.[16]

Ruffer states his impressions of ancient Egyptian dentistry as follows:

The writer's studies have not revealed any facts showing that the Egyptians practised operative dentistry, in fact, the evidence rather points to the conclusion that even extraction was very seldom performed. It is not rare to find in Egyptian cemeteries diseased teeth almost dropping out of abscess cavities, or carious teeth which have caused extensive disease and yet the patient was allowed to die without the relief that would have been afforded by a very simple operation. It is difficult to believe that extractions were not practised at times, but the evidence on that point is nil.

No teeth filled with gold or any other metal have been found. The only set of artificial teeth that has been found comes from a Roman grave, and is deposited in the Alexandria Museum. Clearly it could have been of but little use in chewing and was probably tied in for aesthetic reasons only.

He makes the following conclusions of his studies of the teeth:

1. Among ancient Egyptians, anomalies in position, structure and the number of teeth were rare and did not seem to become more common as modern times were approached.
2. Attrition was, as it is now, very marked, and played probably a considerable part in favouring the entrance of micro-organisms of suppuration, but not of those producing caries.
3. Dental caries occurred in all periods of Egyptian history. It is impossible to say for certain without more extensive statistics whether caries was much less common in ancient than in modern times, but the data from Tourah undoubtedly point to a very small percentage of caries in the Predynastic period. Nothing definite is known regarding the incidence of caries in children.
4. Alveolar and perialveolar abscesses were common at all times in Egypt, and were evidently produced by the same processes as they are now. Attrition played some part in the aetiology of these abscesses, but the majority were secondary to chronic suppurative periodontitis, and a few to caries.
5. Chronic suppurative periodontitis was a common disease in ancient Egypt, and the most frequent cause of the loss of teeth.[17]

An extract from Nielsen's conclusions about the teeth of the ancient Egyptians reads:

It can be confirmed by this skeletal material that caries is not very frequent, but that a very strong attrition and chronic dental abscesses are very common in Nubia. . . . By studying the jaws it is characteristic that the attrition of the teeth in cases of chronic alveolar abscesses has been so excessive that the root often is the only part of the tooth left.[18]

All the foregoing conclusions have been borne out by the author's extensive examinations of dry skulls from all periods of dynastic Egypt, which are housed in various museums and universities of Europe and Egypt.

The one abnormality common in almost every dentition from early childhood onwards, is that of wear of the teeth. Not many authors have expressed views on its cause, apart from the chewing of coarse foods, but Elliot Smith wrote, ' . . . these people ate coarse food, mixed with a considerable amount of sand . . . the teeth rapidly wore down'.

Anyone who has experienced eating food on a windswept desert will not be surprised that mineral particles become incorporated in their food. Thesiger, the Arabian traveller, vividly describes the unpleasantness of consuming rations contaminated with windblown sand.[19]

However, it is obvious that the sand responsible for the constant wear could not have been derived solely from eating on the desert. In order to find an explanation, it was decided to examine all evidence that could offer any hope of revealing the cause. As bread is the basis of meals in most communities, its choice as the first subject of the investigation became apparent. This choice was helped by a paragraph in Ruffer's *Food in Egypt*: which reads:

The most important food of the Egyptians was bread made of various cereals, wheat, barley, and possibly, as well, from lotus seeds and dom-palm dates. The fondness of Egyptians for bread was so well known that they were named '*artophagoi*', or 'eaters of bread'; it was the food par excellence and the word was and has remained synonymous with food in this country. The most terrible curse was 'They shall hunger without bread and their bodies die.'

This investigation was aided by the scenes painted on the walls of a number of the tombs of the nobles at Thebes, the most noteworthy examples being the tombs of Nakht, Menna, Sennedjem and Rekhmire. Methods of sowing grain, and of reaping the corn with a sickle mounted with flint teeth are to be seen, as well as the subsequent beating, threshing and winnowing of the harvested grain.

Since bread was so popular as food, it is not surprising that it was a common practice to place some in the graves of the departed to support life during the hereafter. Pieces of bread have been found in the graves of common people, nobles, and even in the tomb of the Pharaoh himself. Many such pieces have survived and are distributed among world museums, but being of such rarity and interest, samples are not freely available for scientific investigation, more especially if destruction is involved in the process. It was most fortunate that application to some museums had a positive response and the thirteen samples received covered a wide range of both date and site of origin.

A microscopical examination revealed what appeared to be whole grains of corn on the outer surfaces of the bread. In lines of fracture, in a few samples, a cellular structure could be seen, whilst in all specimens there appeared scattered particles of mineral matter which reflected light. An x-ray examination revealed the presence of inorganic fragments and stereoscopy showed that these particles were distributed within the substance of the bread and were not surface contaminants.

The inorganic particles were isolated and a petrological examination revealed that rounded desert grains, mostly quartz, predominated, but grains of feldspar, fragments of amphibole and mica were present; as also were ferromagnesian minerals, probably hornblende and other rock fragments very finely grained, making indentification difficult. The residue from the Turin and Metropolitan museums' samples contained small angular fragments of a greywacke type. The angularity of the fragments suggested a different origin from that of the rounded desert grains.

It is interesting to note that Pliny and other ancient writers refer to the custom of the Carthaginians of adding pounded bricks, chalk and sand prior to grinding corn. The necessity for such procedures was confirmed by A. J. N. W. Prag of Manchester University Museum. Using ancient saddle-stones and querns, he found that after grinding corn for fifteen minutes, the grains remained almost unchanged. When however, the grains were first crushed with a pestle and then one percent of sand added to the sample, fine flour rapidly resulted.[20]

From the foregoing observations it is clear that the mineral fragments in all the samples were derived from the following sources:
(1)   Soil contamination of the grain
(2)   Particles of flint derived from the harvesting tools
(3)   Windblown contamination during winnowing, and storage in the granaries

(4) Fragments derived from the wear of sandstone, limestone and granite saddle-stones and querns, as well as inorganic material added to hasten the grinding process

It seems reasonable to think that the wear of the teeth of these individuals was due to at least three factors, i.e. life in a desert environment, and the consumption of coarse foods and of bread made from flour contaminated with mineral fragments.

It has been recognised that the peoples living along the Nile Valley during the Old Kingdom (c. 2780–2280 BC) were both technically competent and highly developed in terms of art and literature. That they were ready to experiment, exploit and develop new ideas is seen from the change from the use of mud bricks for the construction of tombs and pyramids to the use of huge blocks of quarried stone for the building of vast pyramid complexes. Whilst local stone was mainly used, huge blocks of limestone and granite had to be transported, sometimes for long distances. Alluvial gold from the granite rocks of Aswan was available and jewellers learned to manipulate it and develop their art. Boat building and farming practices had reached a very high standard and the exploitation of natural resources, as depicted on the contemporary tomb walls, had reached a very high level. That the use of writing, based on hieroglyphic signs, was well developed is verified by the abundance of inscriptions on stele and on tomb walls.

It caused no surprise, therefore, when Junker found in the rubble of a tomb shaft two teeth joined together with gold wire, and after specialist opinion had been received, he accepted the judgement that the specimen could be regarded as the work of a dentist, demanding the use of a high degree of skill. The idea of a dental profession received further support when Junker decided that the hieroglyphic sign depicting an elephant's tusk was symbolic of a human tooth and that when it was added to the titles on a stele, it indicated a practising dentist.[21] To this idea additional weight was given by the researches of Jonckheere, who from observing the inscriptions on stele found that there were physicians of the eye, body and teeth.[22]

The result of an examination of an Old Kingdom mandible, showing two holes passing through the outer plate to the apices of a first molar and the report ending, 'The evidence of this specimen seems to establish beyond a reasonable doubt the existence of a rudimentary knowledge of oral surgery in the Old Empire',[23] completes the evidence which aided the growing conviction of medical historians that a highly organised dental profession did exist with its titular head holding a court appointment.

These conclusions are at variance with those of paleodontologists, who collectively have found that the lives of many individuals could have been extended by the very simple operation of removing a few loose teeth. Such is the disagreement that a critical appraisal of the evidence advocating the availability of an organised dental profession is justified.

The instance of the two teeth united with loops of gold wire is cited by all historians as providing evidence of an organised dental profession. This artefact was recovered by Junker from shaft 984 of a *mastaba* tomb at Gizeh. It is now in the care of the Roemer-Pelizaeus Museum, Hildesheim. When I went to examine it (by kind permission of the curator), the two teeth were not united, the twist of wire having fractured. There were however, photographs taken from different angles to show its original condition when it arrived in the museum. An examination of the site of fracture of the wire revealed a central bore, indicating that foil had been rolled in its fabrication. A double loop of wire with part of the uniting twists was around the neck of one tooth, whilst the loop of wire was in the same position around the other one. Absorption of the roots and severe wear of the cusps had destroyed so much morphological detail that identification of the units was difficult. There were no accretions present around the wire.

To summarise:

(1)   The specimen was found, not *in situ* in the jaw, but in the rubble surrounding the skeleton.

(2)   Euler, in his report to Junker wrote, 'Finally, worthy of note, the same in both teeth, are superimposed (stratified) layers on the neck part of the tooth, which were probably there during life and did not just arise subsequently.' Some historians have accepted the foregoing observation as implying that salivary calculus covered the wire (which would be undeniable proof of its human origin) but this is not so. Euler uses the word *wohl* which implies probability, and no mention is made of tartar, but there is reference to layers of an unspecified substance. The theory that its formation was the result of the reaction on the gold wire, by being surrounded by mineral rubble for more than four thousand years, can be accepted with certainty.

(3)   The stability afforded by the loops of wire would have been insufficient for the retention in a living dentition of the third molar almost bereft of its roots.

(4)   The second and third molars are so far back in the oral cavity, that with the cheek on one side and the tongue on the other, to make a twist of several strands of wire between them would be quite impracticable. There is such an obvious and simple way to unite the ends of the wire – on the antero-buccal side of the foremost tooth – that all in all, this artefact cannot be used to support the assumption that the two teeth were united within a living dentition.

When Junker first considered the implications of the two teeth united with gold wire, he accepted it to be an artefact produced during mummification. It was only after receiving Euler's report that he accepted the theory of its *ante mortem* fabrication. His acceptance was facilitated because he acknowledged that the hieroglyphic sign of an elephant's tusk symbolised a human tooth, and thus when conjoined with other signs it was indicative of a simple, advanced or a court dentist.

The hieroglyphic sign of an elephant's tusk was certainly used as a determinative during Middle and New Kingdom times. Doubt has been expressed by some philologists that its earliest use would denote a single and definitive thought, i.e. a human tooth. The settlers of the Nile Valley were acquainted with the African elephant *loxodonta africana* with its gigantic tusks, and it is difficult to accept the argument that in the earliest development of sign writing its exclusive connotation would be the comparatively minute human counterpart. Curiously, the sign disappears from all inscriptions by the end of the sixth dynasty. It is hardly conceivable that if an organised dental profession had existed for more than a century, it would suddenly cease to exist, more especially as the need continued unabated, for Pharaoh and *fellahin* alike. It is much more likely to stand for a court appointment quite unconnected with a healing profession, and which ceased to exist when the country came under a different constitution.[24] Until the results of further study of the royal titles has been made, doubts must be expressed that Junker's interpretation is the correct one.

The observations by Hooton which led him to write that 'The evidence of this specimen seems to establish beyond a reasonable doubt the existence of a rudimentary knowledge of oral surgery in the Old Empire', have been accepted by historians as proof of the existence of an organised dental profession. The statement was based on the examination of a mandible, recovered by Reisner from one of the *mastaba* tombs at Gizeh. It is now in the possession of the Peabody Museum, Harvard University (cat. no. 59303). Through the body of the mandible, in the region of the lower right first molar are two circular holes which communicate with the cavity in the alveolar bone process made by absorption of tissue due to an abscess. The precision and the position of the circular openings caused Hooton to think that they were the results of surgery, carried out by a dentist for the relief of an acute apical abscess. If Hooton had been able to examine all the skulls recovered by Junker and Reisner, he would have found many such examples in both accessible and the most inaccessible areas. An example of the latter is the abscessed pathway leading into the Antrum of Highmore. This can exhibit the most remarkable mechanical precision.

It has been written and accepted by most clinicians that it is not necessary to drill holes in the bone to give relief from the pain caused by an apical abscess, but only to incise the gum and let the pus escape. The process of abscess expansion in itself initiates a sinus path through the outer alveolar plate.[25]

That this particular operation could have been carried out at that period is feasible, because of the availability of flint knives, whose efficiency as cutting instruments can be testified by personal experience. The artifact can be as sharp as a domestic carving knife, but there is no evidence of the availablity of rotating instruments capable of drilling holes in the human frame, nor indeed was there necessity for such tools. Therefore this specimen cannot be accepted as evidence to support the conception of the existence of knowledge of oral surgery at this period.

One artifact, a gold wire prosthesis, has been recovered during recent years by Mr Shafik Farid from a *mastaba* tomb in a cemetery at el-Qatta.[26] The tomb is dated by him to the fourth dynasty, but its extensive re-use during the late periods prevents the acceptance of this device as evidence of dentistry of the Old Kingdom.[27]

Although evidence has been produced by archaeologists and philologists and accepted by some medical historians as proof of the existence of an organised dental profession during the Old Kingdom, this evidence is difficult to accept after a detailed examination. Certainly it is not in accordance with the findings by examination of the human remains. These show that before the age of twenty-five years, the teeth of most individuals gave no problems. The teeth were situated in well developed arches and dental decay was a rare phenomenon. After that age, the wear of the cusps of the teeth initiated such pathological *sequela*, that the well-being and even the lives of some were in jeopardy. Although the various medical papyri record a number of prescriptions for the relief of oral disease, there is no evidence to be seen in the dentitions of the human remains that their use improved or even retarded its progress. On the contrary, in some cases, the attempt to ameliorate the condition resulted in other and ill-fated consequences.

Less than justice would be done to the writer of the Edwin Smith Medical Papyrus if no mention were to be made of case No. 25. The papyrus was written during the Middle Kingdom and describes the technique employed to reduce a dislocated jaw which is an exact description of the method followed today.[28] The reason that this knowledge was available is not difficult to seek. Due to eating coarse foods and foods contaminated with mineral fragments, and to the changed cuspal pattern due to the wear of the teeth, the temporomandibular joints of many individuals undertook wider and wider excursions. The result of this overwork is to be seen in the head of the condyle, where there is sometimes erosion of the cortical bone on all three surfaces, and an altered shape. These changes facilitated dislocation. Examination of collections of mandibles, especially of those in the older age group, reveal that this condition was common. Thus an additional burden was added to those already borne by individuals who needed the services of a skilled and organised dental profession, but examination of their human remains shows that no such help was available during the Old Kingdom and indeed for thousands of years to come.

⟦Part III⟧
FUTURE DEVELOPMENTS

[7]

FACES AND FINGERPRINTS

Two of the techniques which were developed and used in the first phase of the Manchester Egyptian Mummy Reasearch Project were subsequently applied in the field of forensic studies.

Fingerprints

When somebody breaks into a house and leaves fingerprints behind, the routine work of the scene-of-crime officer involves taking the fingerprints not only of suspects and checking them with records, but also those of people with legitimate access to a place, so that they can be eliminated from the enquiry. Living people can turn their fingers this way and that, as guided by the officer in the case. The hands of a murdered person usually can be moved so that fingerprints can be taken to the best advantage. Mummified bodies present different problems.

Asru, the Manchester mummy, was a very special case. The position of her hands meant that much thought had to be given to developing a suitable technique to obtain the prints without disturbing their position. In A. R. David (ed.), *The Mysteries of the Mummies*, an account is given of the materials and method used, but before success came, experiments were made on 'spare' hands and fingers kept in the storeroom of the Manchester Museum.

Close examination through a powerful magnifying glass showed that on one of the spare mummified fingers the epidermis – that is, the outer skin – had separated from the dermis, the under skin, during the period of mummification. The epidermis had deteriorated to such an extent that none of the papillary ridge system – which is what you can see on your own hand – remained.

In his book *Mostly Murder*, the forensic scientist, Sir Sydney Smith reminds us,

It is from the dermis – the underlying, true skin – that the various ridges, loops and whorls that form fingerprints develop. Dermal prints remain after the epidermis has been destroyed by putrefaction or other cause, and they are an equally certain form of identification.

He wrote this in 1959, basing part of his experience on a case in 1935 when Detective Inspector Hammond of Glasgow City Police obtained a dermal print from the body of Mary Rogerson in the famous Buck Ruxton case, still vivid in popular memory. Sir Sydney said the inspector had worked with great skill and the result provided identification of Mary, a servant in the home of the Parsee doctor Buck Ruxton in Lancaster, who had been murdered by him, he having also killed Isabella Ruxton, known as his wife. The evidence was for some reason not given at the trial, thus denying the inspector the credit he had earned.

On the 'spare' finger we were examining, the ridge detail exposed on removal of the epidermis was extremely fine and somewhat damaged but the use of the moulding and casting technique which was developed meant that a very good dermal print could be obtained which could have been readily identified. While we were engrossed in these experiments which enabled the best results possible to be achieved on Asru's hands, it was not expected that the work would be vital in the police investigation of the exceedingly bizarre case of the Rochdale Mummy.

On 15 March 1977, a man's partially decomposed body was found in the refuse area of a block of corporation dwellings in Ashfield Valley, Rochdale. This room was dark, gloomy and ill-lighted. There had been no electric light since a fire in one of the five-foot high bins (used to catch refuse coming down the chutes) had been put out by the fire brigade on 1 March. Because of the smoke the firemen could not say whether the body had been there at the time. On 8 March a woman and her two daughters had seen a wire shopping trolley in the refuse area; on it was a large bundle, which they did not examine, but there was an offensive odour. On 10 March a man saw the trolley in the room; on it was what he assumed was rubbish covered by a dirty sheet, which smelled vile. The caretaker was in the refuse room on 11 March but did not notice anything unusual, and on 13 March, on his next visit, he saw the shopping trolley and what seemed to be a large old sack which he touched. He thought it was a mixture of sand and cement.

On 14 of March he asked the Cleansing Department to send a collecting vehicle so that the rubbish could be moved. The two men who came gave the trolley a push. It struck a piece of wood and then tipped over. The men saw that the 'package' was a partially mummified body, the hands and feet being bound and the head covered with a plastic shopping bag!

The forensic scientists had plenty of material to examine; the body's skin was dried and mummified, and examination of the liver showed death was due to barbiturate poisoning. The plastic bag over the head had rendered facial identification impossible; the 'sand and cement' was in fact millions of mites, and in addition, there were thousands of maggots. Asru was considerably better preserved than this.

Using the technique developed from the work done at the museum on the 'spare' finger, we examined the hands, which had been taken to the Fingerprint Bureau after they had been removed from the body by a Home Office pathologist. On all fingers except one, the skin had deteriorated to such an extent that it was useless; the exception was the right middle finger.

On this, it could be seen that the epidermis had 'lifted' as in the case of the Egyptian mummified finger. With the greatest care this separated epidermis was slowly removed and it was found that the dermis was quite good enough for the application of the new technique. The illustrations (Fig. 7.1) show how, following the rule that there should be no fewer than sixteen corresponding points of identification, we proved to the coroner that the body was that of James Edward Finlay, whose fingerprints were on file.

Enquiries revealed that Finlay had died some eighteen months previously as the result of barbiturate poisoning. His wife, after intensive questioning was committed for trial on two seldom used charges. The first was that she had intended to prevent the coroner of Rochdale from holding an inquest on the dead body of James Edward Finlay, who died an unnatural death or a sudden death of which the cause was unknown, or intending to obstruct the said coroner in the holding of such an inquest, she had concealed the body. The second was that she had left unburied the dead body of her husband, for whom she was bound to provide a Christian burial and had the means of so doing. Both these are offences against common law. Without that vital

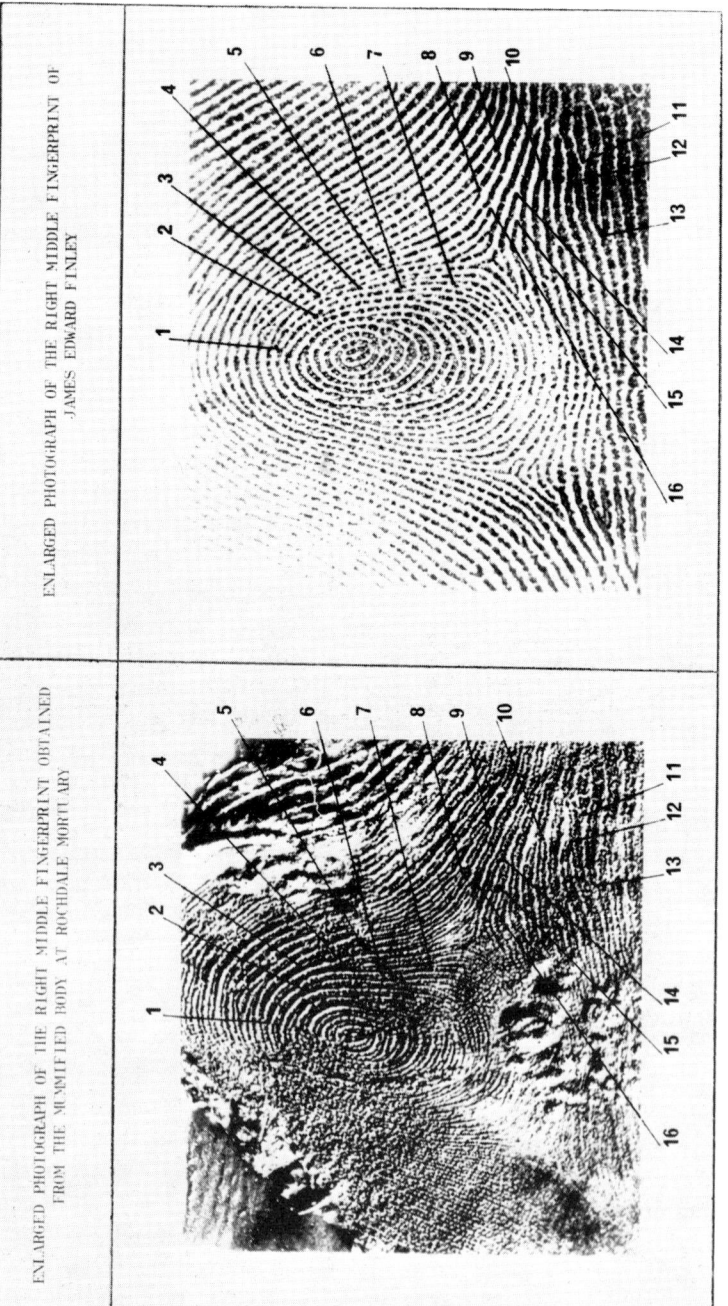

ENLARGED PHOTOGRAPH OF THE RIGHT MIDDLE FINGERPRINT OBTAINED FROM THE MUMMIFIED BODY AT ROCHDALE MORTUARY

ENLARGED PHOTOGRAPH OF THE RIGHT MIDDLE FINGERPRINT OF JAMES EDWARD FINLEY

Fig 7.1 Exhibit prepared for the coroner, showing identification

dermal fingerprint it would have been infinitely harder, perhaps impossible, to identify the body and discover the surrounding circumstances. The woman was sentenced to two years' imprisonment on each charge, the terms to run concurrently.

Most people die in a comfortable bed, whether at home or in hospital and there is not usually the slightest doubt about identity because most people have families and friends. Very few arrange to die violently or indeed untidily; the unknown tramp in a derelict house can slip his hold on life without meaning to be a nuisance, but if he is not found soon, natural decay can make identification difficult. In cases of death by fire, too, it is not always easy to identify the victim, since the exposure to heat has occasionally produced a similar effect to that caused by the mummifying process. As a result of this new technique, now standard practice in Greater Manchester and being adopted in other places, such questions are often easier to resolve.

Not all applications of this new technique have brought about the required result, and there is an interesting example of work done faithfully and well but so far to no avail.

In December 1982, a Mr Baxendale decided to make a dog kennel in the cellar of some premises he had leased in Bolton. His dog Sheba began sniffing round a very dark corner and when Mr Baxendale looked closer, he saw what he thought was a tailor's dummy. Unfortunately, but perhaps understandably, he scooped up the head, popped it into a carrier bag and put it on the counter in front of the duty officer at Castle Street police station in Bolton. This was no tailor's dummy, but the remains of a woman.

As he had moved the head, it was impossible to say for certain whether the woman had been sleeping when she died or had been thrown to the floor. The routine of forensic examination was started and thoroughly carried out.

Parts of this body were mummified, and once again, skilled fingerprint officers made a polysulphide rubber mould from the fingers, covered it with seven or eight coats of acrylic paint (dried very quickly with a hair dryer) and eventually produced three good prints from the mummified right hand and two from the fingers that remained of the left hand. It was a neat bit of work which gave quiet satisfaction.

Checks were made with the National Fingerprint Bureau and at other fingerprint bureaux all over the country. Her fingerprints were not on record anywhere so it can be said that she had not been convicted of a criminal offence. When lying in the cellar her body had rested on some cardboard and newspaper, one piece of which showed it was the *News of the World*, dated 13 March 1966, so it is likely she had lain there since then.

On her body there were rosary beads and nearby was a medallion portraying the madonna and child, making it likely that she was a practising Roman Catholic. Somewhere, somehow, a bible, prayer book or even a diary may come to light, bearing her fingerprints in a condition good enough to compare with those on file with the Greater Manchester Police, and that discovery could lead to her identification. Long experience in police work tells us not to be surprised at anything. Thanks to Asru, some things have become a little more likely.

Facial reconstruction

Few remains of people from ancient civilisations have been more carefully preserved that those of the ancient Egyptians. Because of this preoccupation with preparation for the afterlife, many of their ordinary goods have survived, together with gold and silver jewellery, weapons and a host of other items. Although the embalming process to preserve the body was well practised, the results are seldom of much use when we come to assess the likely appearance of these individuals when they were alive. Archaeologists have been able to give a very graphic description of the daily lives of the Egyptians, and medical science can reveal details of age, state of health, and diet, but the actual appearance of these people remains speculative.

In an attempt to provide this information, to enable these dry and skeletal remains to be more easily recognisable as living individuals, it was decided to attempt to reconstruct the heads of several mummies which were of particular interest. It was recognised that there would be a limit to the authenticity of such reconstructions, but every attempt was made to achieve the highest degree of accuracy. A considerable amount of work has subsequently been carried out in this field, which has supported the claim that the faces thus created are very similar to the true lifelike appearance. Also, advantage can be taken of further technological advances in this field.

The idea that a face could be reconstructed is not new. The earliest recorded work is that of Schaaffhausen in 1877. Kollmann, a Swiss anatomist, and his compatriot, Büchli, a sculptor, were the first to adopt a scientific approach to the problem. Kollmann compiled a series of tables listing the average thickness of soft tissue of the face, and Buchli then sculpted the head and face, using the skull and figures to guide him. These figures remained as the basis for much of the work undertaken in subsequent years, until 1913, when, because of a badly conducted experiment by Professor Eggeling of Jena University, the concept that a face could be scientifically reconstructed fell into disrepute. All work in this field effectively ceased. More recently, the Russian anthropologist Genasimor became an acknowledged expert in the subject, proving to many people that the concept was a valid one. Today, most of the work is carried out in the USA by a relatively small number of people, and it is from here that statistically more acceptable measurements of soft tissue have become available. There is, however, no one way to rebuild a face, and each person works in a slightly different way. Since 1974, when the first head was reconstructed from an Egyptian mummy, the methods have been refined and techniques developed that make the early work seem slightly clumsy. However, it is just as valid, and the basic principles have continued to be applied in the later work.

Of the three subjects chosen for reconstruction, two were of the same date. Unwrapped by Dr Margaret Murray at Manchester in 1908, they had been carefully studied and documented, and it appears that they shared a common mother, but all the evidence suggests that the younger brother, Khnum-Nakht, had a negro father. He suffered from osteo-arthritis which had seriously affected his back, and he seems to have suffered some form of palsy in one foot; the configuration of his front teeth was unusual. The elder brother, Nekht-Ankh, was approximately sixty at time of death, and there is unsubstantiated speculation that he may have been a eunuch. The objective was to bring these individuals 'back to life' as accurately as possible.

First, plaster casts of the skulls were prepared, by using a flexible mould-making compound called algenate and making two part 'split' moulds. Delicate parts of the skulls and the casts were protected from damage because of the flexible nature of the algenate moulds; thus, maximum accuracy of the casts was achieved with a minimum risk of damage to the original skulls. When mounted, these plaster casts were to provide the matrix upon which the heads and faces were made. Using soft modelling clay, the soft tissue of the face, head and neck was built on to the skull. This part of the exercise must be conducted in a very controlled and precise manner, and the depth of the soft tissue is carefully checked to ensure that it corresponds to the measurements established by Kollmann and Büchli. The process of reconstruction is relatively swift; the features and character of the face develop in the early stages and, although the refinements and finishing may continue for some time, the basic details will not change significantly. A number of modifications have been made to the technique since these reconstructions were made, to ensure greater accuracy. Nevertheless, these two heads were quite distinctive and different in appearance. The marked negroid features of Khnum Nakht were particularly striking (Fig. 7.2). It can be argued that the finished heads have a rather blank and cadaverous appearance. This is not surprising since all the measurements of soft tissue thickness were not taken from living people. Moreover, there is no evidence available of the folds and wrinkles in the skin which are so much part of any face.

In this type of work, results are reached by adhering to certain basic rules; to add features for which there is no evidence could be very misleading, although reasonable assumptions are sometimes acceptable.

Two beautifully carved wooden statuettes were discovered in association with the remains in the coffins of the two brothers. There has been some doubt concerning the identification of these statuettes, in determining which figure represents which brother. By comparing the heads of the figurines with the reconstructions, this doubt is quickly resolved for, despite the difference in size, there is now little difficulty in putting the correct name to each statuette. One represents the strong negroid features while the less powerful face of the older man is clearly seen in the second (see Fig. 7.3).

Preceding chapters have already described the condition, age and sex of Mummy 1770; x-rays clearly indicated that the skull had been severely damaged. The full extent of this damage became apparent when, after unwrapping, the skull was seen to consist of some thirty fragments of bone covered in mud and bandages. Most of the bones of the skull were present, and thus it was possible to make casts of each piece in plastic and to reassemble these casts to form an almost complete skull. More pieces were absent from the left-hand side, and there was a defect in the bone in the region of the left-hand side of the nose. The reason for this is not entirely clear, but it is likely to have caused considerable nasal congestion.

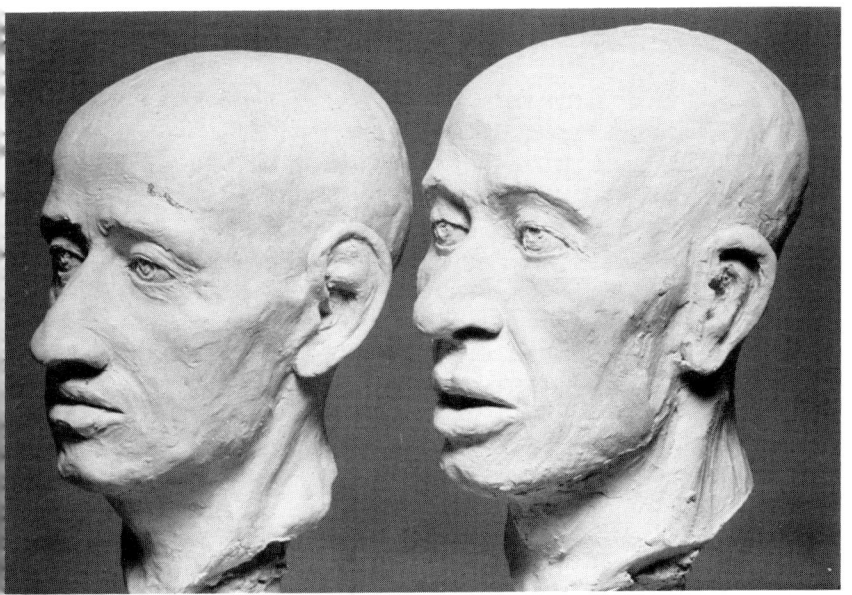

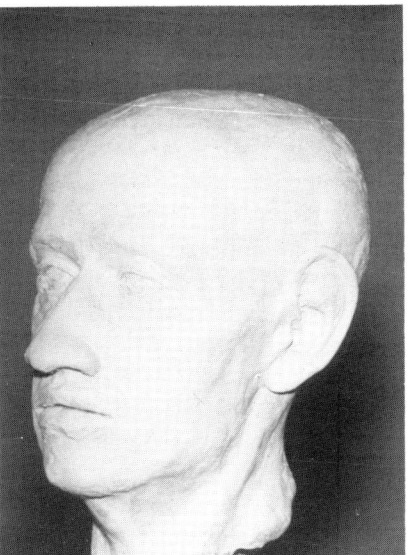
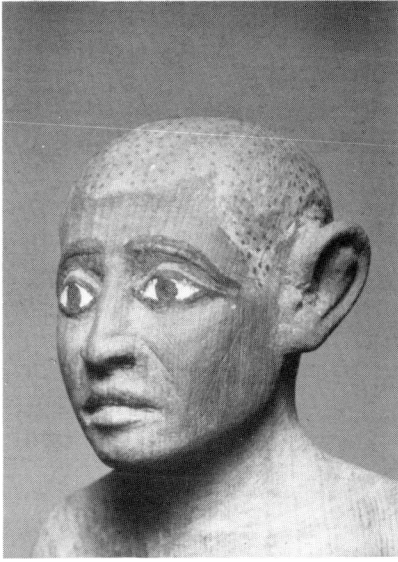

Fig 7.2 Reconstructed heads of the Two Brothers, Khnum-Nakht (right)
and Nekht-Ankh (left)

Fig 7.3 Reconstructed head of Nekht-Ankh compared with small
wooden statuette found in the tomb of the Two Brothers

Areas of the skull that were missing were replaced with wax, but little attempt was made to reproduce fine detail; these were simply included to balance the rest of the skull. A plaster cast was then made of the complete skull into which small pegs were inserted. These pegs were positioned at twenty-three points of the face and cut to a precise length, each peg representing the depth of soft tissue at that point. Previously, measured pegs had not been used, which made it more difficult to achieve accurate measurements (Fig. 7.4). As the face began to take shape, features and characteristics associated with young teenagers were taken into account. Because of the assumed nasal congestion, the mouth was left slightly open, giving her a rather adenoidal appearance. Finally, very minor modifications were made to the eyes and the tip of the nose, and these adjustments were sufficient to change the face into a classic example of an Egyptian. The popular interest in this project was so extensive that it was decided that the reconstructed head of Mummy 1770 should be completed in every detail. Therefore, a wax cast was made of the finished head into which glass eyes were fitted; colour was painted on to the face, and hair and eye-lashes were added. The final effect was strikingly lifelike (Fig. 7.5). Although these embellishments are only reasonable assumptions, they are based on general evidence from the period. Inevitably, there are areas where commonsense must assist a decision, by taking into account the age, sex, build and ethnic group. Subsequent control studies carried out on cadavers show, however, that these reconstructions are far less speculative than might be thought. The test on the cadavers included various stages. First, two cadavers were selected at random by the staff of the anatomy department and were photographed before they were embalmed. When the medical students had completed their studies, the skulls were identified by a number; no reference was made to the photographs at all, and the faces were reconstructed, using the method already described. These reconstructions were then compared with the original photographs, and strong similarities were immediately evident.

All the reconstructions to date have been made on skulls or casts of skulls and, in the past, in the case of Egyptian mummies, this has necessitated the unwrapping of the specimen. New methods are now available and techniques are being developed which will hopefully remove the necessity of having direct access to the skull. An increasing number of skulls of living people are being built to assist in the planning of surgical procedures on patients who are suffering from

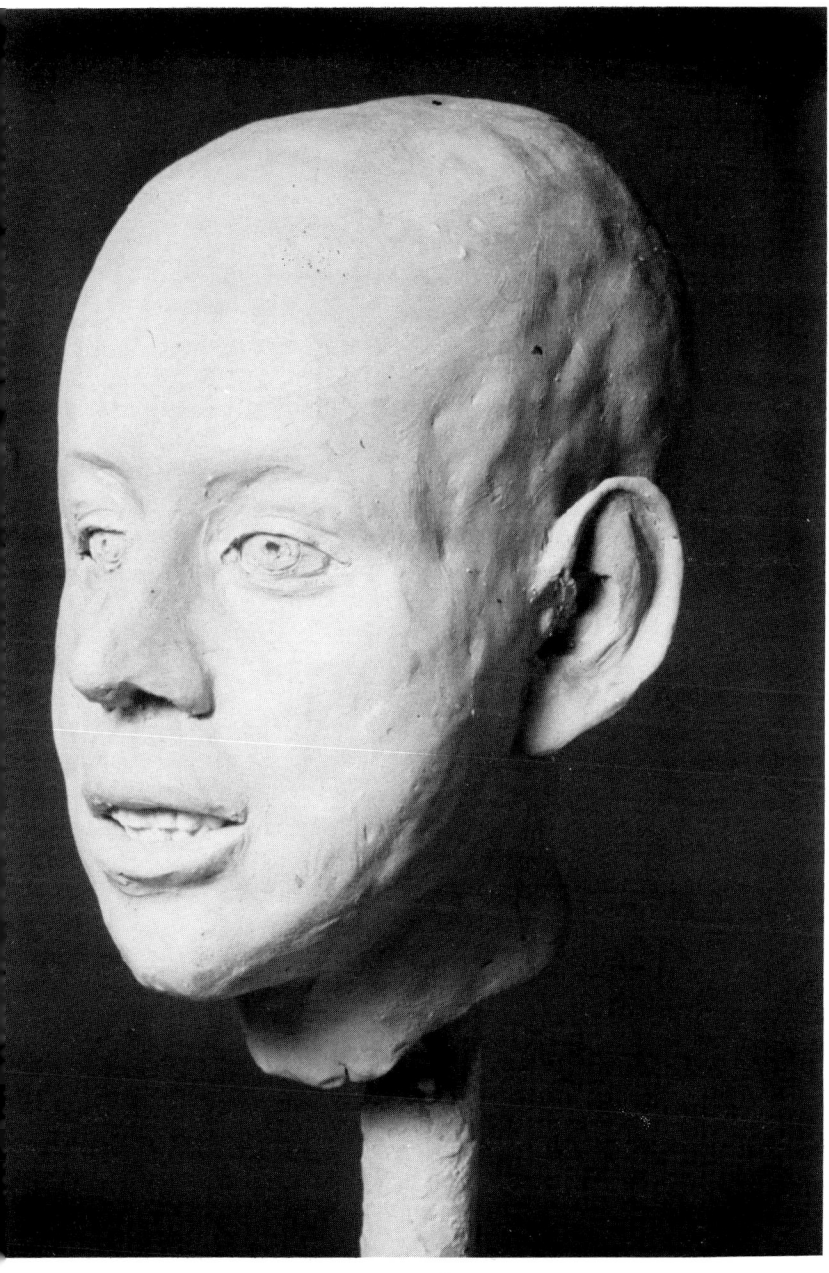

Fig 7.4 Basic reconstruction of the head of Mummy 1770

Fig 7.5 Reconstructed head in wax of Mummy 1770, with glass eyes, eyelashes and wig

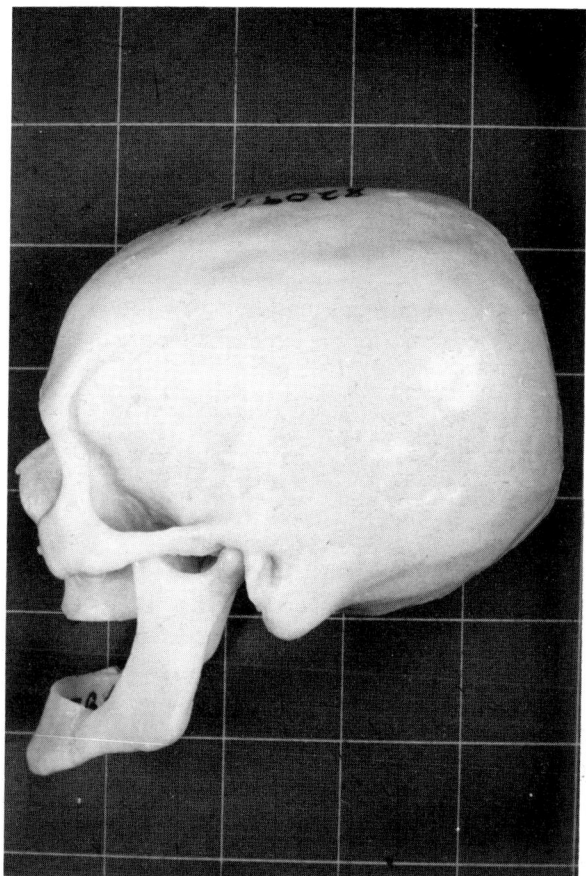

Fig 7.6 Skull reconstruction of patient suffering from malformation of the face

some malformation of the face, either congenital or traumatic, which affects the bone (Fig. 7.6). The modelled skulls are prepared from information provided by very accurate x-rays. These x-rays, or morphograms as they are sometimes called, are made using specialised equipment which,unlike conventional x-rays, enables measurements to be made of the exact size and shape of the skull. It is then possible to reconstruct a face on the model of the skull. A second method which is still being explored involves rebuilding the skull from a series of horizontal x-ray scans. This is more acceptable in many ways, since there are severe limitations in the way in which 'morphograms' can be made with any other than living people. What has been demonstrated is that acceptably accurate models of skulls can be made from x-rays on an almost routine basis, and that to see how a mummy may have looked in life need not necessarily involve destructive procedures.

As the result of the mummy reconstructions, a further development has been the forensic application of these techniques in the identification of otherwise unidentifiable bodies. In both the USA and the USSR similar work is carried out, but until now very little has been done in Britain. The methods used for the forensic subjects are exactly the same

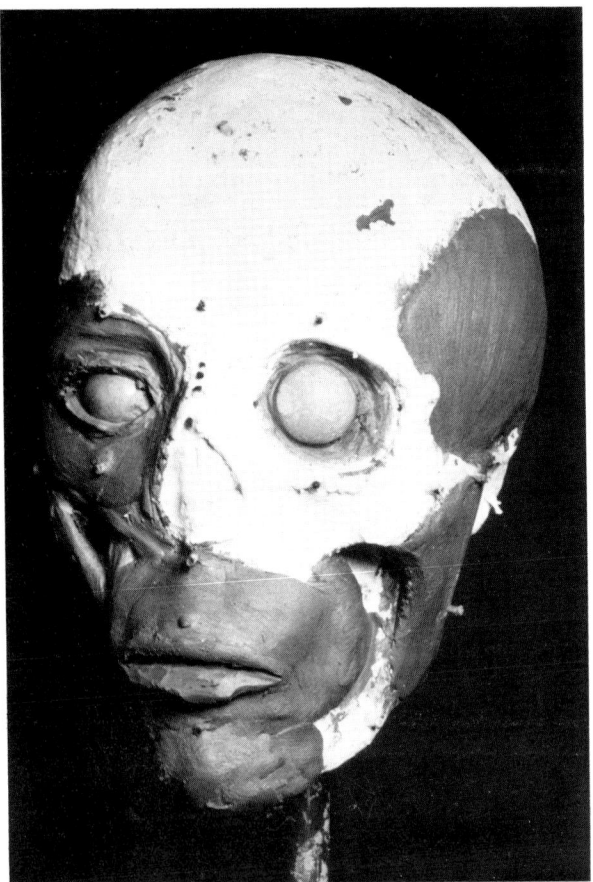

Fig 7.7 Reconstruction of head which assisted in identification of body for forensic purposes

as those employed for the archaeological remains. This has provided the opportunity and stimulus to pursue the work in even greater depth than before. Three cases have been undertaken in recent years and one resulted in a positive identification (Fig. 7.7). Consistency, and a method which relies on as much scientific information as possible are imperative for work of this type to be of any practical value. There are now formulae for making the nose and placing the eyes, and anatomical structure plays a much greater part in building the faces than before, enabling the face to be developed from the surface of the skull outwards.

The idea which was formulated in 1974, to stimulate the interest of those who wished to see the living appearance of the archaeological remains, has achieved considerably more. It is unlikely that, without this original idea, work would have been undertaken either on models or patients' skulls for clinical reasons or on unidentified bodies for forensic purposes. It is particularly gratifying that work carried out on Egyptian mummified remains should have had a practical and modern application.

[8]

ORGANISING THE INFORMATION
THE INTERNATIONAL
MUMMY DATABANK

During one of the sessions of the symposium 'Science in Egyptology' at the University of Manchester during June 1979 the delegates unanimously adopted the proposal to form an International Mummy Data Bank (IMDB) at Manchester.[1] The essence of the proposal was that research on Egyptian mummies had increased dramatically in the past decade or so, particularly in the application to the subject of many modern analytical and investigative methods. Therefore it seemed timely to establish an international repository for all the information that is accumulating, and computerised methods of storage and retrieval were indicated, because of the great volume of this information. It was agreed that the IMDB should be sited at Manchester Museum because it is a recognised centre of Egyptological research that also possesses suitable computing facilities and expertise.

Information gathering

Over five hundred centres worldwide, known or thought to house mummified remains, were circulated during the latter half of 1979, and over 150 replies were received. The vast majority either sent or promised information for the databank, or else gave permission for the necessary information to be extracted from published sources. The 'International' status of the databank is testified to by the fact we have received co-operation and information from institutions in all five continents as well as from several East European countries.

Analysing the information structure

The detailed information on the mummies and their treatment tends to be extremely heterogenous in coverage and presentation and therefore difficult to cross-relate and study. It is the purpose of computerised data processing to structure information formally in such a way that it can be easily indexed, retrieved and presented according to a range of different criteria, without losing the content of the information.

The particular group of data processing programs used by Manchester Museum is called the *Famulus* package,[1] and the totality of information about a given object (or closely associated groups of objects) forms a *Famulus* record.

Within each record the information is broken down into subdivisions called fields; within a field the data may be free-text or structured. The data structure within a field may be defined by controlling the terms that may be entered, or by specifying the items of information to be recorded and their order, or sometimes by a combination of both methods. In addition, the data definition of a field may be recursive, i.e. an information sequence may be repeated several times within a field; an example of this is seen in the treatment of literature references in the field RDOC described below. Where a sequence of items is specified it is necessary also to declare one or more non-alphanumeric characters to 'delimit' the items within the field. When analysing information in this way one must consider both the scope and extent of the information available and, even more important, the probable uses to which it is going to be put.

In the present databank the information is of two types:

(a)   the standard 'catalogue' or 'provenance' information needed to record a museum object: when, where and by whom found, where and by whom now held, a history of events since originally found and a full description of the mummy and attached objects.

(b)   Scientific information obtained by, and needed for, research. This includes critical details of the object's original condition, description and analysis of inscription, the results of invasive and non-invasive examinations and the conclusions therefrom, and information on the use and success of various conservation techniques.

The information about human, particularly whole human, mummies is far more detailed and complex than that usually available about mummified animal remains, and this caused an early decision to build two separate databases for human and animal mummies.

The detailed record and data structure of the IMDB

Famulus requires that each field is identified by a four-character field label; to aid interpretation of output the labels used for the IMDB are as mnemonic as possible. The number, names and order of the fields within a record, together with the definition of the data within each field, including separator characters, controlled vocabulary lists or sequencing keywords, together form the data standard of the databank.

Keywords Because of the heterogenous nature of the information provided for inclusion in the database, the record structure of the IMDB includes several paired fields, one of which contains free text and the other the keywords to rationalise and concord that text.

Keywords or coding terms allow the records to be re-arranged in some specified order when required for indexing purposes; such keywords can also materially assist the selective retrieval of information from the databank. A keyword may be followed by a 'qualifier' (in brackets); if it is judged sensible this combination may be entered again in inverted form e.g. the text 'plates of gilded cardboard material' may give rise to the keywords *Cardboard* (gilded) and *Gilding* (cardboard). So that the information will appear under both main terms in an index. In doublets the keyword lists are appended and can be modified or extended in the light of experience. On the other hand, the original text is always stored exactly as provided by the originating specialist, and it ∴s this full text, with any ambiguities and connotations, that is printed out in any listing of data retrieved from the databank, thus allowing the recipient to exercise their own judgement upon it.

The data categories used in the IMDB data definition

NUFO   The number and form of the principal object of the record, e.g. '1 whole human'

BIOL   Biological attributes of the mummy, structured thus: age in years; sex (method of determination/estimation).

DESC   Free-text description of the mummy and its wrapping, attachments and containers, including information on size and present condition, together with a description of any non-literate inscription.

KEYW   Keywords extracted from the text in the DESC field; the descriptive keyword list includes such terms as *Amulet* (gilded wood), *Sarcophagus* (anthropoid), *Bitumen, Silver* (embalming plate), *Cartonnage* (painted), *Unbandaged, Embalming Plate* (silver), *Wig, Linen*.

LOCY   Site at which found, plus tomb detail.

GCOD   Geographical coding: not in use at present but included in field definition to allow a later grouping or classification of sites.

INSC   Transcription into English of any literate inscription with a note of its position and the method by which it is formed (*Painted* or *engraved*) on the object. The presence of *untranslated hieroglyphs* is also noted here.

ICOD   Inscription keywording: Names of people and places mentioned in the inscription are entered here, with geneaological or other detail added when available. Also coded here are significant inscriptive design elements mentioned in DESC. For example; IRT-IRW (d. of Pedamenope), Dragons (encircling sun), Atum (lord of Heliopolis).

Note that separate indexes can be produced of people, of places and of design elements.

COLN   Act of field collection, structured thus: name of finder, date found, field notes on finding event and/or a cross reference to RDOC field (*q.v.*).

HIST   Free text history of the wanderings, ownership and treatment of the object; may include a cross reference to RDOC field (*q.v.*).

CONS   Keywords referring to conservation treatment received by the mummy, as detailed in HIST.

ACQN   Act of acquisition by the holding institution, structured thus: name of person or institution from which acquired; method of acquisition (this item has a controlled vocabulary: *donation, bequest, purchase, exchange, transferred, other*); date of acquisition; any other detail about the act of acquisition, and/or a cross reference to the RDOC field (*q.v.*).

INST   Country of location and full title of the current institution owning the mummy.

PREN   Previous and present registration or acquisition numbers attached to the object(s).

RDOC   Related documentation, a recursively structured field. If more than one entry is present, each is prefixed with a reference letter to permit cross referencing from other fields. Published citations are entered as [A] and [B], unpublished documents are recorded as convenient, e.g. [C] or [D]; for example, [A] author, date, title of paper one, citation; [B] author, date, title of paper two, citation; [C] 'Bound MS. notebook recording tomb group details in University Library, ACCN. No. 72-9368'; [D] 'Album of photographs of unwrapping kept in Department'.

This field will assist in the compilation of the separate computerised *Bibliography of Egyptology Research* which is in hand.

PERI   Period(s) from which mummy dates

PCOD   Period code, designed to permit chronological ordering of the records, and to assist retrieval either by dynasty or period.

Table 9

Dynasty	Code	Period	Code
		Pre-dynastic 5000–3100 BC	10
I II	11A 11B	Archaic 3100–2686 BC	11X
III IV V VI	12A 12B 12C 12D	Old Kingdom 2686–2181 BC	12X
VII VIII IX X XI	13A 13B 13C 13D 13E	1st Intermediate period 2181–1991 BC	13X
XII	14	Middle Kingdom 1991–1786 BC	14X
XIII XIV XV XVI XVII	15A 15B 15C 15D 15E	2nd Intermediate period 1786–1552 BC	15X
XVIII XIX XX	16A 16B 16C	New Kingdom 1552–1069 BC	16X

Table 9 Con't

Dynasty	Code	Period	Code
XXI	17A	3rd Intermediate period	17X
XXII	17B	1069–522 BC	
XXIII	17C		
XXIV	17D		
XXV	17E		
XXVI	17F		
XXVII	18A	Late period	18X
XXVIII	18B	522–332 BC	
XXIX	18C		
XXX	18D		
XXXI	18E		
		Ptolemaic period	19X
		332–30 BC	
		Roman period	20X
		30 BC–AD 641	
		Islamic conquest	21X
		AD 641 on	

ASSN Associated names, a recursively structured field giving the name of the scholar, institution, expedition or organisation associated in any way with this mummy, excluding those mentioned in the fields COLN, INST or ACQN. Details of the association may follow each name in brackets, for example, EEF (funded finding exploration); Black, Dr E. (assisted at unwrapping, 1927).

EXAM Free text description(s) of examination by different techniques, with an indication of results; usually includes cross references to the RDOC field.

CLNI Classification of Exam field: Keywords include *Biochemical analysis, Blood grouping, Carbon dating, Chemical analysis, Fingerprinting, Histology, Radiology, X-rays (see radiology)*.

MTEC Free text information on mummification techniques usually corresponding to RDOC field.

CLN2 Classification of MTEC field; keywords include *Cavity packing (detail), Arm position (detail), Eyes false, Canopic jars*.

PATH   Free text information on pathological findings, usually with cross reference to RDOC field.

CLN3   Classification of PATH field.

Diseases will be keyworded by name (and synonyms) and also classified by 'nature' from this keyword list:

Infectious diseases, Nutritional factors, Digestive tract, Liver & biliary tract, Kidney & urinary system, Blood & bone marrow, Endocrine system, Genetic factors (e.g. dwarfism), Cardiovascular system, Respiratory system, Connective tissue, joints & bones, Nervous tissue, Skin, Worm infestations, Tropical diseases, Teeth.

ASSP   Associated zoological or botanical specimens.

ASOB   Associated records (i.e. cross reference to other mummies recorded in data bank).

XREF   Cross references to information files held outside the IMDB – e.g. negative numbers of photographs held on file in owning institutions.

NOTE   A catch-all field for information that does not fit easily into any other field.

IDEN   An arbitrary serial number for each record, principally used to assist the computer processing but could also form the basis for an international registration number scheme.

Long term security of the databank

The databank is at present stored on magnetic tape, which is not a secure storage medium, so several copies are kept, some at dispersed sites, and all are checked periodically for readability. It is hoped in the near future that it will be possible to keep a copy of the databank permanently 'on-line' in the computer.

Manchester Museum is committed to the maintenance of the IMDB, and because of the increasing scholastic importance of this databank the Standing Committee of the museum recently resolved that the Manchester Museum should maintain the International Mummy Database, encourage its use for scholastic research and assist in widely disseminating information available from the database, and that efforts should be made to find a suitable alternative institution to accept maintenance in the event that the Manchester Museum was for any reason unable to discharge the above commitments.

Accessing the information

The *Famulus* package contains a very efficient and sophisticated search processor, so that records satisfying complex combinations of criteria can be retrieved easily. Records can be searched for, using any term or terms that may be present anywhere in the record, although naturally, the keyword fields are heavily used in defining searches.

Manchester Museum offers a selective retrieval service to scholars covering its own internal collection databases as well as the IMDB.[2] The service is available free to anyone who wishes to make use of it.

The future

In mid-1983 the databank held information on 233 whole human mummies, but information on additional material is constantly solicited. The databank is dynamic and records will be constantly updated as further details become available.

CONCLUSION

This book records the second phase in the work of the Mummy Project. The continuing interest and involvement of the team members, the acquisition of new material by the museum, public awareness of the results, and the introduction of new, non-destructive methods of investigation have ensured that the project developed. In addition to this book which relates the story of the new researches, another television programme, again produced by the BBC in their *Chronicle* series, has been transmitted, showing how research at the museum, both on the Mummy Project and on a related project concerned with artifacts from a pyramid workmen's town-site, are adding to our knowledge of the everyday existence of the people.

The June 1984 Science in Egyptology symposium in Manchester gave scholars the opportunity to discuss their work and to consider how modern multidisciplinary techniques can help us to understand ancient Egypt. The permanent Egyptology galleries at the Museum are being redesigned and redisplayed and the first phase opened to coincide with the 1984 Symposium; this gallery is based on the theme of Egyptian mummies and the artifacts associated with funerary beliefs and customs, and shows how scientific techniques on the project have been used in this connection. A second gallery will display the museum's outstanding collection of daily life artifacts. Since much material from ancient Egypt has been acquired from burial sites, this collection is of particular importance, to permit a more complete understanding of the society. Here, also, reference will be made to the scientific studies undertaken on this material which adds information on the technology and provenance of some of the finds. Together, the galleries will show how museum collections are not to be regarded as dull stores of excavated material brought out from Egypt many years ago; for the innovative researcher, they are sources of much information which, with modern, multidisciplinary methods, can reveal new facts about the civilisation.

The foundation of the Egyptology collection at Manchester was due to the enthusiasm and generosity of Dr Jesse Haworth, a local textile manufacturer. In recognition of his munificence, but also because of 'his position as one of the first patrons of scientific excavation (as distinct from mere digging for curios or for inscriptions)', the university conferred on him the degree of LLD. Jesse Haworth's aims – to further scientific research in the subject and to make available a fine collection of excavated artifacts to both students and the public – are continued today. Over the past decade, it has been possible to bring together the expertise of many colleagues in the university and elsewhere, and to introduce a programme of multi-disciplinary research on Manchester's Egyptology collection. The future research in this field, both by the Manchester team and by others elsewhere, will continue to contribute to our knowledge. Only by using such techniques and by involving specialists in many disciplines can we hope to build up an accurate picture of the realities of everyday existence in ancient Egypt, which the written evidence alone cannot provide.

NOTES

Notes to Chapter 1

1 A. R. David (ed.), *The Manchester Museum Project* (Manchester, 1979).
2 A. R. David (ed.), *Mysteries of the Mummies* (London, 1978).
3 Quoted in T. J. Pettigrew, *A History of Egyptian Mummies* (London, 1834), p. 3. Everyman's library, (London, 1964).
4 Herodotus, *The Histories*, II, §§ 85–88.
5 Diodorus Siculus. *Bibliothecae Histor.*, I, § 91.
6 Natron is a salt mixture which occurs in natural deposits, with a large proportion of sodium carbonate and sodium bicarbonate, together with impurities.
7 G. Elliot Smith & W. R. Dawson, *Egyptian Mummies* (London, 1924), p. 74.
8 G. Elliot Smith, *The Royal Mummies* (Cairo, 1912), pp. 94–111.
9 Herodotus, *op. cit.*, §§ 90.
10 From Col. Sir Percival Marling, Bt, VC, CB, 'The Nile campaign, 1884–5' in *Rifleman & Hussar* (1931), pp. 162–3. For this information, I am indebted to L. F. J. Walrond, Esq., curator of the Stroud & District Museum.
11 Quoted in B. M. Fagan, *The Rape of the Nile* (London, 1975), p. 45.
12 P. 3.
13 Pettigrew, *op. cit.*, p. 7.
14 Quoted in T. J. Pettigrew, *op. cit.*, p. 11, from *The Works of that Famous Chirurgion Ambrose Parey* (London, 1634), p. 448.
15 G. Belzoni, *Narrative of the Operations and Recent Discoveries within the Pyramids, Temples, Tombs and Excavations in Egypt and Nubia* (London, 1821), p. 156.
16 A. B. Edwards, *A Thousand Miles up the Nile* (London, 1877), p. 51.
17 *Ibid.*, p. 451
18 Given in a summarised version in the foreword by C. D. F. P. Brocklehurst to A. R. David, *The Macclesfield Collection of Egyptian Antiquities* (Warminster, 1980).
19 David, *The Macclesfield Collection*, pp. 20–23.

20 The Director General of the Antiquities Service in Egypt.
21 Clare Sheridan, *Nuda Veritas* (1927). I am indebted for this information to Christopher Hartley, Esq., curator of Brickwall House, Sussex.
22 Pettigrew, *op. cit.*
23 G. Elliot Smith & W. R. Dawson, *op. cit.*, p. 7.
24 Pettigrew, *op. cit.*, p. xv.
25 Elliot Smith, *op. cit.*; Elliot Smith & Dawson, *op. cit.*
26 A. Lucas, *Ancient Egyptian Materials & Industries*, fourth ed., revised and enlarged by J. R. Harris (London, 1962).
27 M. A. Murray, *The Tomb of Two Brothers* (Manchester Museum Handbook, Manchester, 1910).
28 W. M. F. Petrie, *Gizeh & Rifeh* (London, 1907), pp. 12, 27; plates X A–E, XIII E–H.
29 Murray, *op. cit.*, p. 5.
30 W. M. F. Petrie, *Methods and Aims in Archaeology* (London), pp. 180–182.
31 James E. Harris & Edward F. Wente (eds.), *An X-Ray Atlas of the Royal Mummies* (Chicago, 1980).
32 A. & E. Cockburn, *Mummies, Disease and Ancient Cultures* (Cambridge, 1980).

Notes to Chapter 2

1 W. Konig, *14 photographien mit Rontgen-Strahlen, aufgenommen im Physikalischen Verein* (J. A. Barth, Frankfurt am M., Leipzig, 1896); Thurston Holland, 'X-rays in 1896', *The Liverpool Medico-Chirurgical Journal* XLV, (1937), p. 61.
2 W. M. F. Petrie, *Deshasheh 1897, Fifteenth Memoir of the Egypt Exploration Fund* (Egypt Exploration Fund, London, 1898), plate xxxvii.
3 Elliot Smith, *op. cit.*, pp. iii–iv.
4 R. L. Moodie, *Roentgenological Studies of Egyptian and Peruvian Mummies* (Field Museum of Natural History, Chicago, III, 1931).
5 P. H. K. Gray, 'The radiography of mummies of ancient Egyptians', *Journal of Human Evolution*, II (1973), pp. 51–3, and 'Radiological aspects of the mummies of ancient Egyptians in the Rijksmuseum van Oudheden, Leiden', reprinted from *Oudheidkundige medelingen uit het Rijksmuseum van Oudheden, Leiden*, XLV II (1966); W. R. Dawson and P. H. K. Gray, *Catalogue of Egyptian Antiquities in the British Museum*, I (Oxford University Press, 1968); P. H. K. Gray and D. Slow, *Egyptian Mummies in the City of Liverpool Museums* (Liverpool Corporation, 1968).
6 David, *Mysteries of the Mummies*, pp. 109–127.
7 I. Isherwood, H. Jarvis and R. A. Fawcitt, 'Radiology of the Manchester mummies' in David, *The Manchester Museum Mummy Project*; David, *Mysteries of the Mummies*, pp. 149–59; F. F. Leek, 'The dental history of the Manchester mummies' in David, *The Manchester Museum Mummy Project*.

Notes to Chapter 3

1   P. Ghalioungi, *Magic and Medical Science in Ancient Egypt*, Amsterdam, second Ed., (1973), p. 124.
2   E. Tapp, 'Disease in the Manchester mummies' in David, *Manchester Museum Mummy Project*, pp. 95–102.
3   A. Curry, 'The insects associated with the Manchester mummies', in *ibid.*, p. 113–18.
4   I. Isherwood, H. Jarvis and R. A. Fawcitt, 'Radiology of the Manchester mummies', in *ibid.*, pp. 25–64.

Notes to Chapter 4

1   A. Curry, C. Anfield and E. Tapp, 'Electron microscopy of the Manchester mummies' in David, *Manchester Museum Mummy Project*, pp. 103–12.
2   J. M. Riddle 'A survey of ancient specimens by electron microscopy' in Cockburn, *op. cit*, pp. 274–86
3   A. Cockburn, R. A. Barraco, T. A. Reyman and W. H. Peck, 1975, 'Autopsy of an Egyptian mummy', *Science*, CLXXXVII, pp. 1155–60.
4   Murray, *op. cit.*
5   G. Elliot-Smith and F. Wood Jones, 'Report of human remains', *Archeological Survey of Nubia*, Bulletin 2, 1910.
6   D. Morse, 'Tuberculosis' in *Diseases in Antiquity*, ed. D. Brothwell and A. T. Sandison, (Springfield, Ill., 1967), pp. 249–71.
7   A. T. Sandison, 'Disease in Ancient Egypt' in Cockburn, *op. cit.* pp. 29–44.
8   D. Brothwell and R. Powers 'Congenital malformations of the skeleton in earlier man, in *The Skeletal Biology of Earlier Human Populations*, ed. D. Brothwell (Oxford, 1968).
9   Elliot-Smith and Dawson, *op. cit.*
10 A. T. Sandison, 'The study of mummified and dried human tissue', in *Science in Archaeology*, ed. D. Brothwell and E. Higgs (USA, 1963).
11 J. N. Csermack, *Sitzungstgerichte der Akademie der Wissenschaften in Wien*, IX (1852), p. 427.
12 M. A. Ruffer, 'Histological studies on Egyptian mummies', *Memoires de l'Institut d'Egypte*, VI, 3 (1911), pp. 1–33.
13 M. A. Ruffer, 'Note on the presence of 'Bilharzia haematobia' in Egyptian mummies of the 20th dynasty (1250–1000 BC)', *British Medical Journal* I, 16.
14 I. Simandl, *Anthropologie* (Prague), VI (1928), p. 56.
15 A. F. B. Shaw, 'A histological study of the mummy of Har-mose, the singer of the Eighteenth dynasty (circa 1490 BC)', *Journal of Pathology and Bacteriology*, XLVII (1938), pp. 115–23.
16 A. T. Sandison, 'The histological examination of mummified material', *Stain Technology*, XXX (1955), pp. 277–83.

17 J. T. Rowling, *Disease in Ancient Egypt* (MD thesis, University of Cambridge 1961).

18 E. Tapp, 'Disease in the Manchester Mummies' in David, *The Manchester Museum Mummy Project*, pp. 95–102.

19 E. Tapp 'The unwrapping of a mummy' in *ibid.*, pp. 83–94.

20 G. D. Hart, A. Cockburn, N. B. Millet and J. W. Scott, 'Autopsy of a mummy (Nakht-Rom I)', *Canadian Medical Association Journal*, CXVII (1977), pp. 1–10.

21 *Ibid.*

22 E. Tapp, 'Disease in the Manchester mummies', in David, *The Manchester Museum Mummy Project*, pp. 95–102.

23 J. M. Riddle, in Cockburn, *op. cit.*

24 A. Curry, 'The insects associated with the Manchester mummies', in David, *The Manchester Museum Mummy Project*, pp. 113–17.

25 W. E. Evans, 'Histological findings in spontaneously preserved bodies', *Medicine, Science and the Law*, II (1962), pp. 153–64.

26 T. A. Reyman and A. M. Dowd, 'Processing of mummified tissue for histological examination', in Cockburn, *op. cit.*, pp. 258–73.

27 E. Tapp, A. Curry and C. Anfield, 'Sand pneumoconiosis in an Egyptian mummy', *British Medical Journal*, II (1975), p.276.

28 P. Ghaliougui, *op. cit.* (Amsterdam, 1973).

29 *Ibid.*, p. 124.

30 *Ibid.*, p. 125.

Notes to Chapter 5

1 Ghalioungui, (ed.), *Magic and Medical Science in Ancient Egypt*, (Amsterdam/BM Israel 1973), p. 123.

2 J. Blundell 'Observations on transfusion of blood by Dr Blundell', *Lancet*, II (1828), pp. 321–24.

3 K. Landsteiner 'Uber Agglutinationserscheinungen normalen menschlichen Blutes', *Wiener Klinische Wochenschrift*, XIV (1901), pp. 1132–34.

4 A. A. Epstein and R. Ottenberg, 'Simple method of performing serum reactions', *Proceedings of the New York Pathological Society*, VIII (1908), pp. 117–23.

5 A. E. Mourant, and A. C. Kopec, *The Distributions of the Human Blood Groups*, (Oxford University Press, 1976), p. 85.

6 W. C. and L. G. Boyd, 'An attempt to determine the blood group of mummies', *Proceedings of the Society of Experimental Biology and Medicine*, XXXI (1934), p. 67.

7 P. B. Candela, 'Blood group reaction in ancient human skeletons', *American Journal of Physical Anthropology*, XXI (1936), pp. 429–32.

8 A. E. Szulman, 'The historical distribution of blood group substances in man, as described by immunofluorescence', *Journal of Experimental Medicine*, CXV (1962), pp. 977–96.

9 G. D. Hart, M. L. Soots and I. Kuas, 'Blood group testing (Nakht)', *Canadian Medical Association Journal*, CXVII (1977), p. 476.

10 R. C. Connolly, and R. D. Harrison, 'Kinship of Smenkhkare and Tutankhamen affirmed by serological micro method', *Nature*, CCIV (1969), p. 325.

Notes to Chapter 6

1 Herodotus, *op. cit.*, p. 154.

2 David, *Manchester Museum Mummy Project*, pp. 65–77.

3 Elliot Smith and Wood Jones, *op. cit.*

4 Sir M. A. Ruffer, *Studies in the Palaeopathology of Egypt*, ed. R. L. Moodie, (Chicago, 1921).

5 A. J. Wilson, *Signs and Wonders Upon Pharaoh* (Chicago, 1964), p. 81.

6 Elliot Smith, *op. cit.*

7 Harris and Wente, *op. cit.*

8 L. Balout, 'Ramsés ll au Musée de l'homme', *Archéologia*, CXV (1978), pp. 32–46 and 'La momie de Ramsés ll au Musée de l'Homme', *Le Courrier du C.N.R.S.*, XVIII (1978), pp. 36–42.

9 Howard Carter, *The Tomb of Tut-Ankh-Amen*, (London, 1927), p. 155.

10 F. Filce Leek, 'A technique for the oral examination of a mummy,' *X-ray Focus*, IX (1969), 3, pp. 5–9.

11 F. Filce Leek, *How Old Was Tut 'ankhamūn'?* JEA, LXIII (1977), pp. 112–15.

12 H. Junker, *Grubungen auf dem Friedhof des Alten Reiches bei den Pyramides von Gîza*, 12 vols (Vienna, 1929–55).

13 G. A. Reisner, *A History of the Giza Necropolis*, (Cambridge, 1942).

14 W. M. Krogman, *The Human Skeleton in Forensic Medicine*, (Springfield, Ill., 1973), p. 115.

15 E. D. Farmer, and F. E. Lawton, *Stone's Oral and Dental Diseases*, (Edinburgh, 1966), p. 468 ff.

16 G. Elliot Smith, *op. cit.*, p. 279 ff.

17 Sir M. A. Ruffer, *op. cit.*, p. 314.

18 O. V. Neilsen, *Human Remains*, IX (Scandinavian University books, 1970), p. 113.

19 W. Thesiger, *Arabian Sands* (London, 1977).

20 A. J. N. W. Pragg, personal communication.

21 H. Junker, *Gîza*, I., pp. 256–57.

22 F. Jonckheere, 'Les medicins de l'Egypte pharaonique', *La Médecine Egyptienne*, 3, (Fondation Egyptologique Reine Elisabeth, 1958).

23 E. A. Hooton, 'Oral surgery in Egypt during the Old Empire', *Harvard African Studies*, I (1917), pp. 29–32.

24 E. A. E. Reymond, *From An Ancient Egyptian Dentist's Handbook'. Papyrus Vinob D. 12287* (in press).

25 F. Filce Leek, 'Reputed early Egyptian dental operation: an appraisal', in

Brothwell and Sandison, *op. cit.*, pp. 702–5.

26   J. E. Harris, Z. Iskander, and S. Farid, 'Restorative dentistry in ancient Egypt: an archaeological fact', *Mich. Dent. A. J.*, LVII (1975), pp. 401–4.

27   T. G. H. James, personal communication.

28   J. H. Breasted, *The Edwin Smith Surgical Papyrus*, case no. 25 (University of Chicago Oriental Institute Publications, Chicago, 1930).

Notes to Chapter 8

1   *Famulus* is an information storage and retrieval package developed in 1969 by the US Department of Agriculture at the Pacific South West Forest and Range Experimental Station (California); it is now implemented at most UK universities. The name *Famulus* is taken from the Latin term for an assistant to a medieval alchemist, i.e. a 'sorcerer's apprentice'.

2   C. W. Pettitt, *Mandata, How to obtain Information from the Manchester Museum Databases*, Document M1(B), (Manchester Museum, 1981).

SELECT BIBLIOGRAPHY

A. and E. Cockburn, *Mummies, Disease and Ancient Cultures* (Cambridge, 1980).

A. R. David (ed.), *Mysteries of the Mummies: the story of the Manchester University investigation* (London, 1978).

A. R. David (ed.), *The Manchester Museum Mummy Project: Multidisciplinary research on ancient Egyptian mummified remains* (Manchester, 1979).

W. R. Dawson, *Sir Grafton Elliot Smith*, (London, 1938).

W. R. Dawson & P. H. K. Gray, *Catalogue of the human remains in the Department of Egyptian Antiquities, British Museum* (London, 1968).

P. H. K. Gray & D. S. Slow, *Egyptian Mummies in the City of Liverpool Museums* (Liverpool, 1968).

James E. Harris & Edward F. Wente (eds.), *An X-ray Atlas of the Royal Mummies (Chicago, 1980).*

Herodotus, The Histories, Book II.

A. Lucas, 'The use of natron by the ancient Egyptians in mummification' in *Journal of Egyptian Archaeology*, I, 1914, pp. 119–23.

A. Lucas, *Ancient Egyptian Materials and Industries* (fourth ed. revised and enlarged by J. R. Harris) (London, 1962).

M. A. Murray, *The Tomb of Two Brothers* (Manchester Museum Handbook) (Manchester, 1910).

T. J. Pettigrew, *A History of Egyptian Mummies* (London, 1834).

G. Elliot Smith, *The Royal Mummies* (Cairo, 1912).

G. Elliot Smith, 'Egyptian Mummies' in *Journal of Egyptian Archaeology*, 1 (1914), p. 192.

G. Elliot Smith & W. R. Dawson, *Egyptian Mummies* (London, 1924).

GLOSSARY

achondroplasia	a condition of diminished growth of the long bones resulting in dwarfism
adipocere	a fatty substance of waxy consistency into which dead animal tissues are sometimes converted when kept from air under certain conditions of temperature
alveolus	the bony socket of the tooth
antihelminthic	a medicine used in treating worm infestations
Antrum of Highmore	a cavity in the facial bones situated above the roots of the upper molar teeth
apical (adj,), apex (n.)	the tip of the root end of the tooth
autolysis	self-digestion of tissue which occurs when cells die and digestive ferments escape into the surrounding tissues
buccal (adj.)	of the inner surface of the cheek
calvarum	the vault or cap of the skull
cancellous	bone forming a lattice work like a honeycomb
cariogenic	liability to tooth decay
cellulitis	a diffuse inflammation of intercellular tissues
cerebellum	the part of the brain which lies behind and below the main hemispheres of the brain (cerebrum). Chief functions are the co-ordination of fine voluntary movements and the control of posture.
collagen fibres	small fibres arranged in bundles which help to bind together the tissues of the body
condyle	rounded eminence which acts as the joint of the lower jaw
cribiform	a plate of bone at the roof of the nose perforated to allow passage of olfactory nerve fibres
deciduous dentition	first dentition, milk teeth
desmosome	a site of adhesion between two cells consisting of a dense plate, separated from a similar structure in the other cell by a thin layer of extracellular

	material, believed to have cementing properties
distal tibia	that part of the shin bone farthest from the trunk
dorsum sellae	a ridge of bone at the back of the pituitary fossa (*q.v.*)
dura mater	the outer fibrous membrane which surrounds the brain and spinal cord
epiphyses	the end of a long bone separated from the shaft by a layer of cartilage
epithelium	a layer of cells covering all the free surfaces of the body
erythrocyte	a mature red blood cell
ethmoid	a bone at the base of the skull which forms part of the upper bony nose
evisceration	removal of the internal organs
falx cerebri	the fold of dura mater (*q.v.*) between the two cerebral hemispheres
fenestration	a window in the bone
foramen magnum	the large opening in the base of the skull through which the spinal cord becomes continuous with the brain
gingivitis	inflammation of the gums
globulin	a family of proteins forming important constituents of the body
haemolysis	dissolution or destruction of red blood cells
histopathology	the science or study dealing with the cytological and histological structure of abnormal or diseased tissue
hydatid cyst	a cystic space, up to six inches in diameter, resulting from infection with the tape worm *Echinococcus*
hydrocephalus	a condition marked by excessive acccumulation of fluid dilating the cerebral ventricles, thinning the brain and causing separation of the cranial bones
hyperplastic	overgrowth of a part
hypopharynx	that part of the pharynx lying behind the larynx
hypoplasia	defective development of tissue, ie, enamel of tooth
iliac crest	the bony ridge on the crest of the pelvic bones
lipoprotein	complexes or compounds containing protein and lipid
Ludwig's Angina	acute inflammation and suppuration of soft tissues of the neck
mastoid	the process of the temporal bone
mediastinal	the tissues separating the two sides of the chest
menisci	crescent-shaped pieces of cartilage
mesio-angular impaction	forward tilting of a misplaced tooth

nasopharynx	that part of the pharynx which lies behind the nasal cavities
natron	a mixture of common salts found naturally in Egypt
occipital	relating to the occiput or posterior part of the skull
occlusal	masticating surface of tooth
orthognathous	jaws which do not protrude beyond a vertical line drawn from the forehead
osteomyelitis	inflammation of the bone marrow and adjacent bone
osteonecrosis	death or putrefaction of bone
paravertebral gutter	part of the abdominal cavity lying alongside the spinal column
pedunculated	having a stalk
petrous	that part of the temporal bone lying in the base of the skull
pituitary fossa	the space in the base of the skull containing the pituitary gland
periodontitis	degeneration and destruction of the elastic membrane holding the tooth in its socket
proteolipid	*see* lipoprotein
resorption	removal by absorption
sacoiliac joint	the joint between two parts of the pelvic bone
scolice	the head of a tapeworm by which it is attached to the wall of intestine or the inside of a hydatid cyst
sella tursica	*see* pituitary fossa
striated muscle	muscle which, when stained appropriately and examined in histological sections, appears to have bands across the fibres
sulcus	area formed by the soft tissue joining the gum to the cheek
supra-gingival calculus	tartar deposited on the enamel of the tooth above the gum margin
suture	the join between different parts of the skull bones
symphysis pubis	the joint at the front of the pelvis between the two pubic bones
stela	inscribed stone – in Egyptology the term is used to describe a funerary stone, with scenes and inscriptions relating to the life and profession of the deceased and his offerings to the gods
tentorium cerebelli	a fold of dura mater roofing over the posterior cranial fossa
tonofilaments	a structural cytoplasmic protein, bundles of which join cells together

INDEX